# THE BEGINNINGS
## AND TALES
### of
### the LAKE ERIE ISLANDS

*Yours sincerely,*
*Jessie A. Martin*

*Kelleys Island* is an excerpt from *The Beginnings and Tales of the Lake Erie Islands* by Jessie A. Martin.

# THE BEGINNINGS AND TALES of the LAKE ERIE ISLANDS

by
JESSIE A. MARTIN

Copyright © 1990, by Jessie A. Martin

Third printing 1992

*All rights reserved*

Library of Congress Catalog Card Number: 89-82645

# CONTENTS

KELLEYS ISLAND . . . . . . . . . . . . . . . . . . . . . . . . . . . . . . 9

GOVERNOR CELESTE'S HOME . . . . . . . . . . . . . . . . . . . . 33

FAMILIAR TALES OF KELLEYS ISLAND . . . . . . . . . . . . . . 35
    A Tale of Jake Hay . . . . . . . . . . . . . . . . . . . . . . . . . . . . 35
    Three Fishermen Take a Ride on Ice . . . . . . . . . . . . . 38
    The Mascot and the Messenger . . . . . . . . . . . . . . . . . . 40
    The Romance of George Kelley . . . . . . . . . . . . . . . . . 42
    The Tiber River . . . . . . . . . . . . . . . . . . . . . . . . . . . . . . 44
    A Heroic Rescue . . . . . . . . . . . . . . . . . . . . . . . . . . . . . 45
    The Fate of Five Quarrymen . . . . . . . . . . . . . . . . . . . . 46
    A Snowstorm Tragedy . . . . . . . . . . . . . . . . . . . . . . . . 48
    The Disappearance of Elizabeth Selfe . . . . . . . . . . . . 50
    Lost at Sea . . . . . . . . . . . . . . . . . . . . . . . . . . . . . . . . . 53
    Tom Jones . . . . . . . . . . . . . . . . . . . . . . . . . . . . . . . . . 57
    Carrying the Mail . . . . . . . . . . . . . . . . . . . . . . . . . . . . 59
    More Winter Tales . . . . . . . . . . . . . . . . . . . . . . . . . . . 64

| | |
|---|---|
| THE BASS ISLANDS | 71 |
| JOHN BROWN, JR. | 85 |
| NORTH BASS AND MIDDLE BASS ISLAND | 87 |
| GIBRALTER ISLAND | 89 |
| THE FORD TRI-MOTOR | 91 |
| LIFE FLIGHT | 97 |
| THE SMALLER ISLANDS | 101 |
| JOHNSON'S ISLAND | 107 |
| PELEE'S McCORMICK FAMILY | 115 |
| HULDAH'S ROCK | 125 |
| RAID OF THE PATRIOTS | 126 |
| CONCLUSION | 128 |

*KELLEYS ISLAND*

# KELLEYS ISLAND

LAKE ERIE, THE TWELFTH LARGEST LAKE IN THE WORLD, is two hundred and forty-one miles long and fifty-seven miles wide. It consists of 9,930 square miles or 5,097,600 acres of water; 4,990 square miles are in the United States and 4,940 in Canada. It is the oldest of the Great Lakes, the shallowest with its deepest point being two hundred and ten feet, and meanest. There are more ships of all sizes, shapes, kinds, and descriptions on its bottom than any other similar body of water in the new world. It is a lake once seemingly dead, now very much alive again.

The only formation of islands that exists in any of the great lakes is in Lake Erie. Those that are large enough to be named are spread out in the western fourth of the lake. Those in American waters are Kelleys, Mouse, Green, Ballast, Starve, Gull, Gibralter, Rattlesnake, Johnson, Sugar, and the Bass Islands: North, Middle, and South Bass. In Canadian waters we find Pelee, Middle Island, Hen Island, Big Chicken and Little Chicken, the Sister Islands, and North Harbor. It has been recorded that these islands exist because of a great rock bridge which once spanned Lake Erie. They are an extension of Marblehead Peninsula and Catawba Island, which is in fact a peninsula and not an island.

As islands are intriguing to modern man, so they were to our ancestors. The principal differences are up-to-date means of transportation that can bring in tourists at a moment's notice and modern conveniences, shops, restaurants, motels, and entertainment available when they arrive.

The red man and the very early explorers paddled the waters of Lake Erie in the canoe. In 1818 the first steamer ever to appear on Lake Erie was the steamer *Walk-in-the-Water.* Although this was an oddly constructed craft, its appearance was important to the commercial interests of the lake.

There has been much speculation about when and by whom Lake Erie's islands were first discovered. No doubt the earliest visitors were the American Indians, probably members of the Erie, Shawnee, Miami, Wyandot, Delaware, Ottawa, Seneca, and Tuscarora tribes. In 1975, a prehistoric village of the Late Woodland Indians who inhabited the islands over five hundred years ago was unearthed near the Kelley Mansion on Kelleys Island. This archaeological expedition was sponsored by the Cleveland Museum of Natural History and Case Western Reserve University. Although there is some doubt about the authenticity of information, it has been recorded that in 1669, the French explorer and fur trader, Louis Joliet, traveled on Lake Erie, possibly the first white man to do so, and the missionary, Louis Hennepin, who traveled with Sieur de La Salle, said Mass at Middle Bass Island in the later 1600s. In July, 1789, a group of explorers made charts of the Bass Islands and Kelleys Island.

We do know that those islands which are inhabited were settled at various times by people who didn't own the land, beginning in the early part of the nineteenth century. Before the middle of the nineteenth century, the international boundary line between the United States and Canada had been established, alloting almost half of the islands to each country.

Kelleys Island, the largest of the American group, is located nine miles from Sandusky, Ohio, eight miles from the South Bass Islands and three and one-half miles from Marblehead, Ohio. It is made up of twenty-eight hundred acres of land which measures four square miles. Its shoreline is nearly eighteen miles long.

A trader named Cunningham lived on Kelleys Island before 1800, and for this reason it was first known to the white man as Cunningham's Island as well as Island No. 6. This man had no legitimate claim to the land. The state of Connecticut had retained a strip of land forty to sixty miles wide running one hundred and twenty miles west from Pennsylvania to the eastern boundaries of Seneca and Sandusky counties. This strip of land encompassed the Lake Erie Islands. In 1794 the Connecticut Land Company had formed to sell this land. Many Indian tribes also claimed the land, but in 1805 they relinquished their claim.

Irad and Datus Kelley, sons of Judge Daniel Kelley of Middletown, Connecticut, had migrated to the Cleveland, Ohio, area and often sailed from Cleveland to Detroit and back. Thus, they became acquainted with the islands. By August 31, 1836, through the Hon. John W. Allen of Cleveland, who was an agent for the Connecticut Land Co., the Kelley brothers had purchased all but ninety-one acres for $4,475.06. They later acquired the ninety-one acres, invited people to buy acreage from them, and began a community. The first deeds were issued to Addison Kelley, who was Datus Kelley's son and land agent, Horace Kelley, Bernard McGettigan, Patrick Martin, John Titus, J.E. Woodford, and James Hamilton. In 1840 the name of Cunningham's Island was changed to Kelleys Island.

In 1809 the island became a part of Danbury Township in Huron County, Ohio. From 1837 to 1840, it was a part of Danbury Township in Erie County, Ohio. Then from March 6, 1840, to December 31, 1845, it was a part of Ottawa County as Kelley Island Township. Finally, on January 1, 1846, Kelley Island Township was transferred back to Erie County. On July 27, 1887, Kelleys Island was incorporated as a village, which it is today.

Addison Kelley had five children, all born in the same house. But because of the shifting of the island from one county to another and from one township to another, three of his children were born in Kelley Island Township, Ottawa County; one on Cunningham Island, Danbury Township, Erie County; and one on Kelleys Island, Kelley Island Township, Erie County.

The first religious services held on the island after the arrival of the Kelleys took place on November 9th, 1837. The Rev. Mr. Crane, an Episcopalian clergyman from Cleveland, presided at the service. After this date a Mr. H. Bicksford and

Datus Kelley held services of singing hymns and reading sermons.

During the summer of 1862, a Protestant Sunday School was organized by some women who were vacationing at the Island House. After summer had ended and vacationers had left, islanders continued this Sunday School for the benefit of their own children. It was formally organized in 1863 as the "Union Sunday School" with Mr. M.K. Holbrook serving as Superintendent.

The first church building erected on the island was completed by the Catholic congregation in 1863. Prior to 1861, priests came from Port Clinton and Sandusky to hold services in a private home, probably that of Henry Lange.

In 1861, Kelleys Island was organized as a Station. The first priest to serve this station was Father Louis Mouton from Holy Angel's Church in Sandusky, Ohio. His successor was the Rev. Mr. George A. Verlet from Port Clinton. Under Father Verlet's guidance, in 1863 the Catholics built a small stone church on a lot donated by Henry Lange. This was St. Michael's Church. Twice in its history it has been enlarged, and on November 7, 1915, the Church, which had been almost totally remodeled and refurnished, was re-dedicated. Father Verlet served until May of 1865. He was replaced by Father Charles Kuemann and then a succession of other priests.

One of the interesting landmarks on Kelleys Island today is the old stone church standing on Division Street. In 1865, a German Reformed Congregation Church was organized, and two years later the members built and dedicated a church from stone quarried on its own property. The first minister to this church was a Rev. Mr. Kness; the last resident minister to serve was the Rev. Mr. Von Kaske, who served in 1871, at which time there were twenty-five members. Other ministers held services there, but they served other churches as well. The church is no longer used for worship services. It is now the headquarters for the Kelleys Island Historical Association, whose members are working diligently to restore it and maintain it as a historical landmark.

When Town Hall was dedicated in 1860, Mr. Kelley stipulated that "every creed and doctrine should be allowed a hearing within its walls." Consequently, many religious activities of various faiths have taken place there. In 1865, some island Protestants began to meet in Town Hall. This group of worshipers used the services of the Rev. Robert McCune as their pastor.

Mr. McCune was an army chaplain at Johnson's Island during the Civil War. While there, at various times he visited Kelleys Island to officiate at marriages and funerals. On September 10, 1865, he began preaching regularly in the Town Hall. On March 4, 1866, this group to whom he preached formed the Union Evangelical Church, the first Protestant English-speaking church on the island. It boasted a membership of thirty-four islanders who by November 27, 1877, had built and dedicated a church of their own. It was located across and down the street from the present Zion United Methodist

*The Zion United Methodist Church at the corner of Chapel and Division Streets. It was built in 1893-1894.*

Church. When the church was completed, the town's library was moved from the Town Hall to the church's basement and was eventually run by the Young People's Association of that church.

In the Fall of 1868, a Mr. Holbrook, who had worked under the leadership of Mr. McCune and had been ordained a minister, became the regular pastor. At this time the members joined the Congregational believers and changed the name from Union Evangelical to the First Congregational Church of Kelleys Island. Eventually the church discontinued services, and in 1933 those who were still members gave their building and property to the community church, which is the present Zion United Methodist Church at the corner of Chapel and Division Streets.

This Methodist Church has been through many changes since the island's early history. In 1854 there was a small class of worshipers who used the German language. In 1873 this group built a small church which is still standing but is now a private home. It is the first house on the same side of Division Street north of the Methodist Church. In 1875 they were sent a resident minister, the Rev. Mr. Theodore Suhr, from the Evangelical Association. By 1910, the English language replaced the German in worship services.

In 1934-35, the church building was remodeled, and the present educational rooms were added. Most of the building material for the remodeling came from the Congregational Church. The present altar was once the organ in the Congregational Church.

This Protestant Church outgrew all the other Protestant churches on Kelleys Island, and by the middle of the year 1942, it was the only Protestant church holding services. Although it has often been referred to as the Community Church, it was never officially named that. From the beginning it was known as Evangelical. In 1946, the Evangelicals joined the United Brethren's faith, and the church was named the Evangelical-United Brethren, more commonly called the EUB Church. Then in 1973, this union joined the Methodist organization.

During the days when quarrying and grape growing were

active industries on the island, there was a Greek Catholic Church located on Division Street. As of this writing in 1985 there are only Zion United Methodist and St. Michael's Churches.

When the Kelley's first arrived on the island, there were no schools. In 1836, Miss Lucretia Wood, the island's first teacher, taught ten pupils. In 1837, the first school house, a little frame house located on Division Street, was built. The teacher for this was Miss M.H. Dean. In 1850, District School No. 2 was built on the east end of Woodford Road. In 1853, a large two-story stone building replaced it. In 1865, the graded system began, and a Mr. Holbrook taught a "select" group in the base-

*The only Kelleys Island school building now in use. Officially named ESTES SCHOOL, it was built in 1901. The erection of the building began when James Estes bequeathed the sum of fifteen thousand dollars toward a new school.*

ment of Town Hall. From 1867 to 1870, a school for the German residents of Kelleys Island was taught in the basement of Town Hall, also. In 1877, a frame high school building was erected on Division Street near the center of the island. Not far from this site, in 1901, a new brick high school building was built, and in 1985 is still standing and being used as the only Kelleys Island School. It houses grades kindergarten through twelve, though there may be years when there is only one high school pupil. At one time there was a Roman Catholic school on the island as well as some others which have all passed into history.

In the 1960s, Kelleys Island's citizens voted to become a member of EHOVE, a new vocational school, funded and used by three counties—Erie, Huron, and Ottawa. This is located in Erie County near Milan, Ohio. When Kelleys Island's pupils reach the eleventh grade, they are eligible to attend EHOVE, if they so desire. The local school board pays airplane transportation to fly them back and forth to the mainland on a daily basis. As population decreases and there are fewer young people on the island, the high school's future is uncertain at this writing.

Although there is a municipal water system, even today there are many cisterns, surface wells, and deep wells servicing people on Kelleys Island. Early islanders drew their water from Lake Erie. Draymen hauled barrels of water on wagons and similar vehicles to those living inland. Later windmills were erected along the shores, and tanks were built from which water flowed through pipes to nearby homes. Gasoline engines then replaced the windmills.

At one time the Kelleys Island Lime and Transport Company owned and operated a limited water works system. This, however, didn't fulfill all the islanders' needs for water, so in 1935 the Kelleys Island Water Board was formed. Lee Brown, Orville Lange, and Charles B. Martin served as the first board members. During August of 1935, Erie County Engineer Mr. Harold Gerold presented plans to the Village for the island's new water system. The WPA (Franklin D. Roosevelt's Works Progress Administration) laid about three miles of water mains, and the following year forty customers were ready to receive service. This same water system now owns about eight miles of water lines and services more than two hundred customers.

During Louis K. Starkweather's term as mayor of Kelleys Island from 1965 until the end of December, 1973, he began negotiations with government bodies to build a water filtration plant. As water was pumped directly from Lake Erie and treated with chlorine gas to purify it, many residents felt that it was not one hundred percent pure. Although Mr. Starkweather didn't live to see his filtration plant built, he was instrumental in laying the basic foundation for financing the project. During the Spring of 1974, the first spade of earth was turned to begin the plant; during the second week of December of that year, water, filtered and chlorinated in the new $300,000 water treatment facility, began flowing to homes throughout the island.

Underwater cables conduct power from Marblehead to a station not far from the main ferry dock, from where electricity travels to the farthest points on the island. The electric company is a co-operative owned by Hancock-Wood Electric Co-operative, Inc., of North Baltimore, Ohio. In 1953, islanders formed their own Lake Erie Electric Co-operative, Inc. Later this group merged with Hancock-Wood. Lake Erie Electric Co-operative purchased the Martin Power and Light Company, which was the only company supplying power from 1939 until 1953.

Ohio Service was the first company to supply electric power commercially to Kelleys Island. This company was sold to Buckeye Power and Light, who in turn sold out to a man in Pennsylvania. The Pennsylvanian in turn sold to Fred Martin, whose ancestors were among the first island settlers after the Kelleys. He operated the company from 1939 until his death in 1945. His family continued the company until 1953 when islanders formed the co-operative to get a more adequate supply of electricity.

In 1964 a new electric co-operative warehouse and office building was constructed on Lake Shore Drive, not far from Neuman's Boat Dock. This not only serves the people engaged in the electric business but also houses the present post office.

Kelleys Islanders were able to communicate with the mainland after a telegraphic cable line was laid by the steamboat *Gazelle* on June 19, 1875. The land line was completed a few days later, and so on July 8th, the first actual communication took place. This same cable was used for both telegraph and telephone messages.

As time has passed, changes have taken place in the communications system between the island and the mainland. There is no longer a telegraph service. Telephone service is about as reliable on the island as it is anywhere else. In June of 1974, islanders were able to use the direct dialing system for which they expressed much gratitude as this meant a noticeable reduction in their telephone bills.

Kelleys Island is rich in limestone which had a reputation of being superior to any other in the market in the 1800s. At one time there was a lime kiln on the north side of the island from which lime was transported. Quarrying on the island actually began before the Kelleys purchased their land. Before 1830, a man by the name of John Clemons had operated a quarry and built a dock on the north shore, where Division Street would end if it were extended all the way to Lake Erie. Although this quarry was apparently abandoned around 1835, others were opened on various parcels of land near the west and south shores. William S. Webb, George W. Kelley, A.S. Kelley, George C. Huntington, and Charles Carpenter are some of the early settlers who owned and operated their own quarries.

At that time stone was sold by the cord, a cord being equivalent to five and a half tons. As docks had been built and used for shipping both cedar wood and stone, many boats were able to dock at the island to purchase stone. Then boats usually carried from fifty to sixty cords of stone.

Limestone from Kelleys Island was at first sold for building. It was used to build both the Cleveland, Ohio, and Cedar Point breakwalls, as well as the Cleveland High Level Bridge. The first large American lock at Saulte Ste. Marie, Michigan, was built with Kelleys Island stone. Flux stone used in pig iron or blast furnaces was quarried and shipped and became almost as important a product as the building stone.

On May 14th, 1865, Franklin and Norman Kelley purchased all the quarries and docks owned by William S. Webb and A.S. Kelley. This was the beginning of the consolidation of the Kelleys Island quarries. Then, in 1891, the Kelleys Island Lime and Transport Company absorbed most of the stone business on the island.

In 1924, all the quarries except the North Side Quarry, which Glacial Grooves overlooks, merged into one immense opening extending from the west bay to the east for over a mile.

For nearly fifty years the Kelleys Island Lime and Transport Company quarried stone and furnished a livelihood for several families. In the year 1910, the island's population was 1,017 people. In 1940, for many reasons—outdated steam equipment too costly to replace, changes in raw material demands for the steel industry, and costly shipping—the company ceased its operations on Kelleys Island. This was, indeed, a setback to the island's economy.

For more than twenty years, the quarry land remained idle. It was useless except for the occasional hiker and fossil hunter searching for trilobites, cephalopods, and gastropods.

In the early 1960s the Breckling Company of Cleveland purchased some of the quarry land that was idle, and in 1965, quarry operations began again on Kelleys Island. This was probably the shortest operating period of the island's quarry history under one company, as the Breckling Company soon sold its holdings. Finally a Levy Brothers' Company from Detroit, Michigan, which operated under the name of Kellstone, Inc., concluded that history. Because of labor problems and some misfortunes with company owned freighters, in 1972 operations again stopped. Later in the seventies some quarrying resumed, but that ceased, and only large, gaping holes in the ground remained.

Lake Erie's islands are well known for excellent bass fishing in the water surrounding them. Although we have no records of commercial fishing at Kelleys Island when the Kelleys first arrived, we do know that in the 1830s and 1840s, whitefish, black bass, large pike, and muskellunge were marketed from the area around Kelleys Island.

Mr. Charles Carpenter was an early settler who appeared in several different phases of the island's history. He came to the island in 1843, and on November 7, 1844, he married Caroline Kelley, the daughter of Datus Kelley. So far as is known, this was the first marriage occurring on the island. We know that Mr. Carpenter owned and operated a quarry. He was also active in the grape and wine industry. He assisted Mr. F.R. Elliott in organizing the fruit and floral department of the first Ohio State Fair at Cincinnati, Ohio. He was also in charge of a fish hatchery which the Ohio State Fish Commission established on the island in 1877 for the propagation of black bass and whitefish.

In the early history of Kelleys Island, commercial fishermen set and lifted their nets from "pound" boats. These were usually flat bottomed, straight sided, centerboard sailboats, about thirty-five feet long, having two sails. If there was no wind, the fishermen rowed their boats out to their nets, or "pounds." The pound was a net trap at the end of a long lead net, usually twenty feet wide and from a quarter to a half mile long. Pound stakes, thirty to forty feet in length, were driven by a pile driver into the bottom of the lake, and nets were attached to these stakes. Fishermen lifted their nets every day or so to remove what fish they'd caught. Later, trap nets and gill nets became more useful.

In 1906, Lay Brothers Fishing Company from Sandusky, Ohio, was the first to use a boat with an engine for commercial fishing in the area. For many years this company had a fleet of boats and employed Kelleys Islanders to fish for them. During the 1940s and 1950s, after the quarry had closed, most of the island's "bread winners" earned their living by commercial fishing. When Lay Brothers ceased operations at Kelleys Island in the 1950s, most of the island's families moved to the mainland.

For a few years some of those fishermen who were left on the island operated their own rigs under the name of the Kelleys Island Fisherman's Co-operative. In 1964, some of them were still catching pickerel, but it wasn't long before they, too, weren't plentiful. The price of the abundant perch reached such a low level that it was no longer profitable for the Co-operative to remain in business. Now there are no commercial fishermen on Kelleys Island.

Datus Kelley introduced the first grapes to Kelleys Island in 1842 when he brought a few grape roots with him from his home in Rockport. The first roots and cuttings were Isabellas and Concords. His son-in-law, Charles Carpenter, developed the first possibilities of growing grapes commercially when he planted a vineyard of Catawbas near the road on Lake Shore Drive just west of Sunset Point in 1844. Two years later five dollars worth of grapes were sold. Seventeen years later, the entire grape crop on Kelleys Island brought $51,080.00. In 1870, the crop brought $150,000.

George Huntington made a barrel of wine in 1850, trying to in some way dispose of his surplus crop of grapes. After this, in 1854, several German families from the wine districts in Germany migrated to Kelleys Island to engage in grape culture and wine making. Later some Russians, reported to be refugees escaping military duty in the Russian Army, located on Kelleys Island specifically to work in the vineyards and wineries.

Charles Carpenter built the first wine cellar in 1851; it was the first one to be built north of Cincinnati. In 1860, the Kelleys Island Wine Company was organized and built the largest cellar ever built on the island, completing it in 1872. Its capacity was 500,000 gallons of wine. Three times this cellar met with disaster. It caught fire on September 1, 1876, but it wasn't demolished. After being rebuilt, it burned again in July 1915. Once more it was restored, but again, for the last time, burned in August 1933.

At various times in the 1800s and early 1900s, there were at least twenty-four wine cellars operating on Kelleys Island. Many of these became homes and are now being used either as year-around homes or as summer cottages. One would never recognize the buildings as wineries. Some fell into decay for lack of care. Others burned.

Grapes were considered the most valuable product of the island between 1860 and 1875. The wines produced from these grapes gained national attention and were considered superb by wine connoisseurs. Unfortunately, all of this came to an end. Several things caused a decline in the grape and wine industry on the island—prohibition, competition with California wines, cost of replacing worn out vineyards, higher costs of labor, plus a lack of interest and knowledge manifest in a new generation of people. Although there might be interest in reviving the wine industry, the availability of land doesn't exist. Too much of it has been turned into building lots.

The tourist business probably began on Kelleys Island in 1846 when the steamboat *Islander* was put into commission. It made trips three times a week between Sandusky and Kelleys Island. When companies operating passenger ships between Buffalo and Detroit learned of the *Islander's* schedule, they often took passengers aboard and left them at a Kelleys Island dock.

Datus Kelley's house was the only island house large enough to accommodate more than two or three people, and so he was obligated to be host for the unexpected traveler dropped off by the passenger ships. He didn't charge the "guests" for room and board in those days.

As demands for accommodations grew, a three story addition was built onto the Kelley's original house. It was called the Island House, the first hotel of any importance on any of Lake Erie's islands. It opened for business in the Spring of 1853 with Addison Kelley and his wife in charge. In 1862 and again in 1865 it was remodeled. Unfortunately, on November 2nd, 1877, the Island House was destroyed by fire.

Fishing attracted fishermen; grape crops brought buyers; summer weather brought families, and so a necessity arose for other accommodations. One of the interesting hotels in which many tourists stayed still stands on Lake Shore Drive not far from the Inscription Rock. This is known as the Himmelein House. It was first erected as a family homestead in 1849 by John and Johanna Himmelein.

The son of these two, Mr. John Himmelein, was an advance agent for repertoire groups in show business, and he brought several acting companies to the island during the summer. He added another story and more rooms to the center section of the house, making it the size it is today, and he used it as a hotel for the acting companies. It opened in May of 1890. It had its own dock and beachhouse on the shore and a bandstand on the front lawn where summer concerts were held. At one time it hosted United States Presidents Grover Cleveland and William Howard Taft, who came to the island for bass fishing. In 1920 when the Himmeleins no longer cared to operate the business, the hotel closed and once more became a family homestead.

For a time the transient summer visitor gave way to the cottage owner. During the 1940s and 1950s, most of the "summer people" either came to spend the summer in their cottages or came as a visitor to one of the summer homes. The few hotels and tourist homes that accommodated guests usually had people who came for a week or longer. Not many came for an overnight visit.

In the late 1950s a spot of land on the south side of the island known as Kelleys (later Hummel's) Pond was developed into a marina under sponsorship of the Cruse Company Corporation. This was reportedly a half-million dollar project boasting an eleven hundred foot basin with a three hundred foot breakwall and one hundred eighty-six slips for boats. In 1960, named the Seaway Marina, it opened for business, bringing a different kind of tourist to the island, the boater. Some of the boats coming into the marina were equipped with sleeping facilities, and these brought families or friends for lengthier visits. Others came for short visits to restaurants and bars. There were financial difficulties, and the marina ceased operating under the Cruse Company Corporation. For several years it has operated under different managers and various owners. It is generally acknowledged that the marinas have been responsible for changing the basic character of Kelleys Island.

In the late 1950s and early 1960s, a few other changes came to Kelleys Island to bring more tourists who came for short visits. One big boost to tourism came when the Neuman Boat Line built a dock at Marblehead, Ohio, in 1955 and purchased an open-deck, diesel powered ferry boat, the first of its kind with both ends open to be used on Lake Erie. Later it moved its operation from the old store dock on the south shore of Kelleys Island farther west to where it is located as of this writing. The summer boat schedule is accommodating and permits the tourist to come to the island for a few hours, see the attractions, and make the return trip to the mainland all on the same day.

In 1963 a state park opened on the north side of the island. After the State of Ohio had acquired from the Village of Kelleys Island in 1968 a strip of sandy beach bordering the park, outdoor camping on the island really "boomed." The park opened with only fifteen campsites; within a few years' time it was servicing more than seventy thousand visitors each summer season. There are presently camp rentals, which consist of a tent with dining fly, cots, sleeping pads, a cooler, a picnic table, a fire extinguisher, a propane gas stove, a battery-operated lantern, a throw mat for the tent entrance, a broom, and a grate for cooking over an open fire, all for one fee.

*The Casino, a popular tourist spot, and the old Dock Company, where the Chippewa and other boats brought in many tourists.*

There are two high points of interest that Kelleys Islanders are proud to show to the visiting tourist: Glacial Grooves on the north side of the island at the junction of Division Street and Titus Road and Inscription Rock on the extreme south side on Lake Shore Drive. Both attractions are owned and protected by the Ohio Historical Society.

Geologists have said that the grooves are the longest and finest examples of glacial scorings in our Western Hemisphere. They measure four and a half miles in length, thirty-six to forty feet in width, and penetrate solid rock about seventeen feet. They were carved about twenty-five thousand years ago during the last Ice Age. Huge granite boulders at the base of glaciers passing over the northern part of the United States scraped through the soft limestone plateau of the island, leaving the grooves we see today. Some of the grooves were at one time quarried for their limestone.

In February of 1923, Ed Knopf transferred a small parcel of land containing glacial grooves to the Cleveland Museum of Natural History. Today this parcel of land is maintained by the Ohio Historical Society. In October of 1967, it was dedicated and entered in the National Registry of Natural Landmarks by the National Park Service of the United States Department of the Interior.

For years the grooves went unprotected. Children climbed over them and played on them. Visitors often brought chisels and left Kelleys Island with chips of the grooves in their pockets for souvenirs. In recent years the rare value of Glacial Grooves was realized, and steps were taken to preserve and protect them. During 1973 and 1974, more of the grooves were uncovered. A fence and steps were placed around the entire area so that the observer can see and admire but not touch. He can also get a magnificent view of the abandoned north quarry as well as Lake Erie as it stretches out to the north and east.

Inscription Rock has been entered in the National Register of Historical Places by the National Park Service. From approximately 100 A.D. to 1654 A.D. Erie Indians inhabited the area including Kelleys Island, and the stone carvings found on the rock are attributed to these Indians by some authorities. Others attribute the pictographs to the Mound Builders.

The rock was first discovered (after the Kelleys had come to the island) by Mr. Charles Olmstead of Connecticut. He was visiting in 1834. The "find" was reported to government authorities in Washington, D.C. Captain Eastman of the United States Army was directed to the island to make copies of the rock as well as to map the island for the Bureau of Indian Affairs showing Indian village sites and mounds. His drawings were published in 1852 in a six volume work edited by Dr. H.R. Schoolcraft.

The rock is a thirty-two by twenty-one foot limestone boulder. When it was first discovered, the inner end of the rock was partially buried. Within thirty years the bank had washed away a space of about twenty-five feet, leaving the rock completely exposed.

For more than a hundred years after its discovery, Inscription Rock was badly treated by the weather, the bather, and children at play. Today it's almost impossible for the casual observer to trace or interpret the pictographs. In 1967 the Ohio Historical Society constructed a cover which offers protection against any further erosion.

There are many interpretations of the pictographs by various authorities. According to the opinion of one scholar who believed the writings to be that of Erie Indians, the inscriptions are divided into three sections. The lower section shows a figure of wisdom, a Sachem in charge of records and agreements made in councils, a figure under the protection of the Sachem, and a figure representing a conquered tribe. The middle section is comprised of representations of birds and animals, possibly intended to represent a sanctuary for men, birds, and beasts from the Gulf of Mexico northward to the Great Lakes. There are no weapons. Human-like figures seem to indicate the smoking of a peace pipe and the burial of a battle axe. In the top section there is another Sachem who is a custodian of the sacred Calumet or Pipe of Peace. All other figures in this section symbolize peace. Thus, the tale told indicates a record of a peace agreement among Indians between the Great Lakes and the Gulf of Mexico.

Another historian wrote that the pictographs told the story of the destruction of Erie Indians before the white man set foot in this territory. The Eries controlled the southern shore of Lake Erie and would not permit passage through it. However, they were conquered by the Mohawks and driven out in the middle of the 1600s. This historian does not state whether the Eries might have carved the tale or whether the Mohawks did.

In 1964 one descendent of the ancient Mound Builders asserted that Indians weren't at all responsible for the carvings but that the Mound Builders were. According to his interpretation, the writings on the rock hold many secrets and symbols of the ceremonials and worship services of his people. He believes the inscriptions have some connection with Serpent Mound, which is located in Adams County in southern Ohio.

The sign posted by the Ohio State Historical Society near Inscription Rock tells us that the meanings of the petrographs are not known. Evidently this is the most accurate opinion of all.

Not far from Lake Erie on the east side of Division Street stands Town Hall. This building is the center for many of Kelleys Island's civic and social functions. The hall was a gift to the community from Datus Kelley and his wife Sarah Dean Kelley. Constructed of limestone quarried on the island, it was dedicated to the community by the Kelleys on October 26, 1860, although a deed to the property was not transferred until after Mr. Kelley's death in 1866.

The hall has been used without charge for many activities. The island's first high school began in its basement. It housed the first public library on the island. The first Protestant English Church on Kelleys Island held its services there. Memorial services, graduation services, elections, town meetings, basketball games, bake sales, bazaars, parties, dramatic functions, and dances have taken place there. This building is one monument left by the Kelleys that has truly served the community.

Across from Inscription Rock on the corner of Addison Road and Lake Shore Drive sits a lovely mansion of stone. Though not the oldest house on Kelleys Island, it is without doubt the most interesting. It has been called the "Old Kelley Home," the "Dominican Camp," and the "Kelley Mansion." It was built during the Civil War period from 1861 to 1865. It was a wedding gift from Datus Kelley to his son Addison. For half a century it was one of the showplaces of northern Ohio because of its spaciousness and luxurious furnishings.

The main point of interest in the home is its circular staircase. This was built of a solid piece of dark oak about twenty feet high. Its steps were tied together in some mysterious fashion in groups of three. It is self-supporting with not one single nail used in its construction. Although this story has been refuted by some, it has been said that Mr. Kelley had met an Englishman in New York City who had built such a staircase, and he asked the Englishman to build one for the Kelley Mansion. It was built in London and hauled in sections to the island by boat. The staircase leads upward to a "widow's walk," up to an attic and a rotunda. A lone window in the attic overlooks Lake Erie. Under the rotunda in the attic floor is a skylight that overlooks the staircase.

The beams, woodwork, and door frames of the mansion are solid mahogany and cedar. Special shutters were built on the inside of the windows to protect them from lake storms and the weather. They fold back into the woodwork when they are open. The ceilings are high with ornate plaster work around them. The exterior is of native limestone with cement pedestals and lofty pillars adorning the front.

The Dominican Sisters of Adrian, Michigan, purchased the Kelley property in 1933. For twelve years it served as a retreat and educational center for the Sisters. Then in 1945, they opened it as a summer camp for girls. During the twenty-seven years that it was in operation as a camp, more than eight thousand girls from ages six to fourteen attended from many different parts of the world. There was a a program for them of canoeing, crafts, horseback riding, and even a swimming pool, in spite of the vast swimming area in front of the house. In 1972, because of a decreased enrollment and lack of adequate financial backing, the camp closed. In 1974, the Sisters sold the camp to a family.

Although the walls of the house have seen many children over the years, there was only one baby born there. That one was the late Captain Frank Hamilton.

Kelleys Island is an ideal place for campers. During its

history a variety of camps have experienced years of activities on its lands. Some have become nonexistent; others have grown until they are almost villages unto themselves. Such is Camp Patmos, which islanders often refer to as the Baptist Camp.

Camp Patmos is located on the northeast part of the island, the main camp area on what was once Robert Hamilton's property. It sits on twenty-eight or more acres with lake frontage on both the east and north shores. The main building is called the Villa.

An organization called the Ohio Regular Baptist Home and Camp, Inc., a group within the Ohio Association of Regular Baptist Churches, purchased this property in August of 1952 from V.A. Choloupka for a sum of twenty-two thousand dollars. Father Choloupka was a Roman Catholic priest who had owned the Villa for several years and had used it as a camp for troubled boys. When the Baptists purchased the property, there were four cabins plus a dormitory on the upstairs floor of the Villa.

At an annual meeting of Ohio Regular Baptist Home and Camp, Inc., in October of 1956, Brother Elton C. Hukill made a motion to build one new cabin each year. The motion carried. There are now enough cabins to serve thousands of campers each summer.

In 1958 and again in 1971, John Morse, owner of property adjacent to the camp, donated serveral acres of his land to the camp. Also in 1971, a lighthouse was installed on the north shore in front of the Villa, two cabins were built, and plans were made to add a dining room with shake trim to the front of the Villa.

The Finley Memorial Chapel, named in memory of Dr. H.K. Finley, was built near the stone wall known as Old Image on the north end of the property and was dedicated in individual group services during the summer of 1959.

In 1968, a swimming pool was completed at the camp. It is forty feet by eighty-one feet with three diving boards, one a three-meter board and the other two, one-meter boards. This was not only a fine addition to Camp Patmos but has proved to be an asset to Kelleys Island citizens, who are invited to use the pool and enjoy the fellowship of Camp Patmos on Saturday afternoons during the summer months when camp is in session.

Another active camp on Kelleys Island is the 4-H Camp located on Ward Road on the northern part of the island. The history of this 4-H Camp goes back to the year 1944, when the Sandusky County Extension Agent, B.W. Reading, found ten acres of overgrown farm land, trees, and buildings for sale on Kelleys Island. The land's one asset was a sand beach that bordered Lake Erie. Unfortunately, Mr. Reading couldn't get other counties to share his enthusiasm except for Erie County.

In April of 1945, incorporation proceedings for the camp were completed by citizens of Erie County, and in May of that year, the incorporators deposited four thousand four hundred seventy-five dollars with George Beatty, who took first mortgage on the property. In 1946, the farm people of Erie County collected ten thousand dollars, which paid for the land and everything on it, including a house, a barn, and a 1921 touring car. The house became a dining room; the barn, a recreation hall; and the money left after the purchase was spent for tents, bunks, mattresses, and cooking equipment. In 1947, fifty young people made use of the camp.

In 1948, ten adjoining acres were purchased from the Kelleys Island Lime and Transport Company. Growth was slow because of limited funds. People interested in farm youth lent helping hands to build needed cabins, a new dining hall, and to make improvements and repairs. By September of 1957, the camp was ready for dedication, the climax of which was an ox roast with an invitation to all islanders to attend and feast. The Governor of Ohio was to be the main speaker, but last minute commitments caused him to send a replacement.

Just as in any other community, the island's business places come and go. In the past there have been confectioneries, a meat market, a feed store, a dock company's store, billiard halls, barber shops, blacksmith shops, and once there was a bowling alley.

According to records, the oldest business building on the island is the bar called "Matso's Place" on the corner of Division Street and Lake Shore Drive. The first general store was built on the dock at the south end of Division Street around 1838. Addison Kelley was the first storekeeper. The store housed the first post office on the island. As it was too small and inadequate for the island's growing population, in 1850, George Kelley built a new building on the northwest corner of Division Street and Lake Shore Drive. At that time the business was not a bar or a saloon, but it was a general store.

This particular store was referred to as "the Lodge," home of "The Independent Order of Island Loafers." As this was the only central place for early islanders to meet, it was an active place where the men played checkers and discussed the politics and problems of the day. Ownership of "the Lodge" passed to several different people, including Erastus Huntington, Titus Hamilton, Frank Reinheimer, the Murphy Brothers, and Joe Matso.

Kelleys Island's post office has seen many different homes since its origin. Its first home was the general store at the foot of Division Street; then it moved to "the Lodge." From there it went next door to the store that was referred to as "the Corners." Then it went to the east side of Division Street next to Town Hall to what most residents recognized for years as Brown's General Store Building. On September 6th, 1974, it moved to the Electric Co-operative warehouse.

A visitor or casual observer pays attention to a business-place only to the extent that it supplies his need. However, a resident sees the business as a vital part of his community. Many businesses on Kelleys Island have seemingly sprung up overnight only to die just as quickly. Although ownership of others may have changed from time to time, some have become an established and welcomed part of an islander's life, giving him the individual contact he needs to survive isolation.

# GOVERNOR CELESTE'S HOME

UPON ARRIVING AT KELLEYS ISLAND, MANY TOURISTS ask, "Where is Governor Celeste's home?" In July of 1985, Governor Richard Celeste purchased a ninety-two year old house located on nine acres of lakefront land near the airport on Kelleys Island's east shore. He paid $177,500 to Cleo Starkweather for the property.

Cleo and her husband Louis migrated to the island from Canal Fulton, Ohio. He was a retired executive from B.F. Goodrich, and he later served as mayor of Kelleys Island for eight years. They purchased the property in the 1950s. Paul Beltz, a former mayor, and his family had lived in the house.

The house was built by William Becker, an immigrant German grape farmer, in the early 1890s. The stone used to construct the fireplaces and foundation were quarried on the island. Most of the rooms were large, with high ceilings. The Starkweathers did some remodeling and refinished the house twice. They added electricity, oil heat, baths, and closets and furnished the house with antiques that were family heirlooms. They placed hand-hooked rugs made from old woolens on the hardwood floors.

Mr. Starkweather passed away in 1974. Although Mrs. Starkweather lived in Sandusky, Ohio, most of the year, she continued to maintain the house until the Celestes purchased it. She left some of her treasured antiques for them.

The house is ideal for the Celeste family of the governor, Dagmar, and their six children: Eric, Christopher, Gabriella,

Noelle, Natalie, and Stephen, as well as any others who might come into the family. It's large enough, comfortable, pleasant, and in a private location and is perfect for use as a vacation home.

# FAMILIAR TALES OF KELLEYS ISLAND

ONE OF WEBSTER'S DEFINITIONS OF A TALE IS "A STORY or account of true, legendary, or fictitious events." Often in the re-telling of a tale, it loses certain elements of truth, or it gains different dimensions. So it is with some of the stories that follow. However, some have been reported in newspapers and magazines and are re-told based on documented evidence. Relying on similar incidents or based on stories he might have heard, the reader will need to use his own judgment on what part of the story is fact and what is fiction.

Most of the stories told about Kelleys Island as well as the other islands of Lake Erie concern the water surrounding the land or conditions of the weather caused by the water. That lake is the Boss of the islander's way of life. Whether it's winter or summer, it tells him when he may come and go, and if he doesn't listen, he might find himself in trouble.

## A Tale of Jake Hay

One of the most fascinating tales of adventure about an islander concerns one versatile man by the name of Jake Hay. By trade he was a carpenter who made boats, oxen yokes, whiffle trees, sleighs, wagons, wagon wheels, cupboards, gates, coffins, and almost anything else that was necessary for pioneer living.

It's been said that there isn't a foot of Kelleys Island land that hasn't borne the imprint of Jake Hay. He knew every stick of timber on the island and where to get it.

He was a temperate man who probably never said an evil word against his fellow man. He had a special affinity for children, and his carpenter's shop was one of their favorite stopping places for handouts of candy. As no one is perfect, he had one weakness, tobacco.

Jake owned land purchased in 1855 on the lake west of Inscription Rock. Here he built a dock, which extended about ten feet into the water. Near the center of the dock he built a flight of stairs for the convenience of the public who hauled their water from the lake. At the east end of the dock, he built his carpenter shop; at the west end, a blacksmith's shop, which he rented out. As Jake was a slow worker, those who didn't want to wait for him were welcome to use his tools and shop to do their work themselves.

Jake was a bachelor until 1872 when he married Ellen Pallen. They had three children. Tragedy befell them when their only son was killed accidentally when he was ten years old.

Jake was originally from Cleveland, Ohio. In 1835 he went to Pelee Island where he was employed as a woodchopper for a sawmill. He stayed there for a winter without enough provisions and nearly starved. He left Pelee, headed for Sandusky, Ohio. However, the boat on which he sailed went no further than Kelleys Island (Cunningham Island at that time). While waiting for a chance to get on a boat going to Sandusky, Jake worked for Addison Kelley, who was building the scow, *Argus*.

At this time a Patriot Army, who were in reality rebels against the Canadian Government, visited Kelleys Island. They tried to persuade some of the island men to join them, but Jake convinced the islanders that joining the rebels wasn't a very smart idea, and so no one went with these Patriots.

While Jake had lived on Pelee, he planted eight acres of wheat. When he left, he hired a Mr. Conklin to harvest this crop, and so in February of 1838 he went back to Pelee to collect for his grain. He remained there five days. On his return trip to Kelleys Island, the Patriot Army passed him on their way to invade and plunder Pelee inhabitants.

Nearly seven months later Jake again went to Pelee Island. When he arrived, he was accused of being with the Patriots when they raided the island the winter before, and the inhabitants of Pelee were determined to hang Jake. They confiscated his rowboat, but he escaped by swimming to Middle Island, a distance of nearly three miles to the south.

A man and a boy who lived on Middle Island gave him shelter, but they refused to take him to Kelleys Island. The preceding year Jake had abandoned a dugout canoe because of a split in one end. He sawed off the split end, and nailing a board across, he made it tight enough to stay afloat with continual bailing. He paddled for Kelleys Island with nothing but a broken board, hoping to reach shelter before an approaching storm hit. With less than a mile to go, the storm did come, sweeping Jake and his canoe down the lake. He broke loose a thwart or two and lashed them in the bow to form a cross. As he bailed water with an old nail keg aboard, he removed his shirt and hung it on the cross with the arms through the sleeves, thus making a sail. Then he used the board with which he'd been paddling for a rudder. He bailed constantly as the gale blew all day and all night.

On the second day he saw no land. At dusk the wind carried him toward the shore of Avon Point near Cleveland where huge waves dashed against the rocky shore. Knowing that his crude craft could be broken to pieces, he steered it away from this shore on down the lake.

By morning the storm had abated. People watching from shore saw the man in the strange boat paddling feebly toward them. They helped him ashore and took him to a nearby farmhouse at Dover Bay. After hearing his story, they took him to the home of Chester Dean a few miles away at Rockport, near Rocky River.

After a few days rest at the Dean residence, Jake walked to Cleveland where he was able to get passage on a boat bound for Sandusky, Ohio. He soon learned that the captain and his crew were drunk, and so Jake and a young woman passenger (whose husband was drunk, too) navigated the boat to the Huron River. At this point, Jake abandoned ship and walked to Sandusky. There he was able to get a boat to Kelleys Island.

As he had been gone for two weeks and everyone assumed he had drowned, all were astonished and delighted to welcome him home and hear the strange tale he had to tell.

## Three Fishermen Take a Ride on Ice

Most islanders are active people and enjoy outdoor sports such as swimming, boating, fishing, and hunting. When winter arrives and Lake Erie is frozen hard enough to carry a man with his shanty, ice fishing becomes king of sports. Little villages of shanties spring up in one day's time.

The fisherman uses a small wood, canvas, or metal building containing a place to sit, some kind of heating device (usually a charcoal, kerosene, or gas stove), and with one end of the floor open through which he fishes. He goes armed with creepers to enable him to walk on the ice, a spud for digging a hole, some minnows for bait, hook and line, and enough lunch to fortify him until the evening meal at home. The fisherman's day is usually a long one if the fish are biting.

Sometimes, if the weather stays cold and the ice is good, the sportsman will leave his shanty in the same position for several days. However, if there's an off shore wind blowing, or if the temperature rises drastically, he'll pull his shanty to the beach each night for fear of losing it.

A person not educated in the sport of ice fishing has been known to say, "You wouldn't catch me out there on that ice." Be he stranger or veteran, anyone who ventures out on Lake Erie ice should be cautious. Those who have lived on the lake respect it and usually know whether or not it's safe to be on the ice. Nevertheless, there is a strong current in some of the water around the islands, and even the most experienced sometimes run into trouble.

So it was with three Kelleys Island fishermen who went out to try their luck one Sunday morning in the 1960s. Other islanders who normally would be fishing were in church. This was a time when the prized pickerel were scarce, although there were plenty of perch. These three men decided that the ice was good enough and that if they went far enough north, they might be able to pull in a walleye, as the pickerel are most often called.

After fishing for a couple of hours or so, they had caught no pickerel but did have a pail full of perch and decided that was enough fish for the day. As it had proved to be a good perch spot, the ice there was thick, and there was hope for pickerel another day, they left their shanties and walked in toward the beach. Much to their surprise, after going a few hundred yards, they came to open water. They were on an ice floe which had broken loose and was floating down the lake. Looking to the east, they saw a field of ice jutting out from Long Point into the northeast bay of the island. They decided that if their calculations were right, the floe would join the field of ice, and so they didn't become too concerned. The floe did soon join the field. However, they weren't able to walk to the beach as they'd expected to do because the field had also broken loose and again they faced open water. There was nothing to do but to stay where they were. Fortunately, a young man who had attended church that morning rode back to the north side to see what the fishermen were catching. When he saw their predicament, he located a rowboat on the beach, went after the men and brought them safely to shore.

The men didn't lose their shanties because the current stopped running, the ice stayed where it was, and in a few days the open gap was again frozen enough for them to return to their fishing spot for more perch before they dragged their shanties home.

# The Mascot and the Messenger

Many boats have serviced Kelleys Island since the coming of the Kelleys, but none for a longer period of time nor more faithfully than those owned by the Neuman Boat Line of Sandusky, Ohio. This line was established in 1907, although islanders didn't use its service regularly until a few years later.

John P. Neuman owned a boat works at Sandusky. In 1911 he built a gasoline powered motor vessel fifty-two feet long, fifteen feet wide, with a five-foot draft, and he named it *Reliance*. This boat was used to carry freight from Sandusky to Kelleys and the Bass Islands and to tow "live cars" of fish from upper Sandusky Bay to the fish houses at Sandusky.

In 1920 the *Reliance* was sold, and the following year Mr. Neuman's boatyard built a gasoline-powered wooden vessel named the *Messenger*. This boat was sixty-five feet long, 15.8 feet wide, with a draft of five and one-half feet. In the spring and fall when regular steamers weren't hauling passengers to the islands, John Neuman scheduled trips with his *Messenger*. In summer he used her for charter trips to the islands as well as to Detroit and Toledo. She also towed a barge that carried automobiles back and forth to Put-in-Bay. During prohibition she carried grapes and grape juice from island wineries to Detroit and Cleveland. She also carried workmen to the islands to cultivate vineyards and harvest their fruit.

In 1923 the *Messenger* was converted to diesel power. As she was such a busy boat, in 1925 Mr. Neuman built a similar diesel-powered, sixty-five foot wooden vessel, which he called the *Mascot*.

The *Messenger* and *Mascot* towed barges of coal to heat island homes. They hauled gasoline for island tractors and trucks. They continued scheduled runs to the islands in spring and fall and charter service in summer until 1939. After that time, as the big steamers were no longer making their regular trips to the islands, these two boats gave full time, scheduled service throughout navigation season.

All went well with these faithful two until December 11, 1929. Pelee Island, Ontario, had sent out a distress call for coal and gasoline. The *Mascot* answered this call and, loaded with all the gasoline drums and coal she could carry, ventured out through the rough waters of Lake Erie. She was safe until she left Sandusky Bay. When she reached the open lake, her cargo shifted, and she went to the bottom.

The *Messenger* was running her regular passenger and freight schedule to Kelleys Island just ahead of the *Mascot*. Fortunately, her captain saw what had happened and was able to rescue three crew members and two passengers aboard. But he couldn't rescue her.

In 1930 the *Mascot* was raised and rebuilt. She continued service until 1947, at which time she went into limited towing and charter service. In 1955 she was sold to the Key-Erie Boat Line of Cleveland, Ohio. For five years she lay in the Old River

*Mr. John P. Neuman's* Mascot, *built in 1925 and continued in service to the islands until 1947.*

bed of the Cuyahoga. Twice she sank at her moorings. Her end came in 1960 when she was buried at the river bank, covered with tons of fill dirt.

In 1947 the *Messenger* was sold to the Welch Line at the Soo. She proudly performed her job of taking tourists through the Soo Locks until she was decommissioned and broken up at Sault Sainte Marie, Michigan, in 1958.

Several other boats, the *Commuter (I* and *II)*, the *Challenger,* the *Corsair,* and the *Kelleys Islander,* all larger and more sophisticated, have plowed Lake Erie between Sandusky or Marblehead and Kelleys Island for Neuman Boat Line. But none have been spunkier or shown more spirit than Mr. John P. Neuman's *Mascot* and *Messenger.*

## The Romance of George Kelley

Irad Kelley, one of the original Kelleys who first purchased Kelleys Island, had a son named George. Although George didn't arrive on the island until 1847, in 1843 he purchased land from Addison Kelley. This parcel of land consisted of one hundred forty acres of lot number six.

George and his father went to Tennessee to buy sheep, and while there they stayed at the home of one Colonel Eastland. George became very ill and stayed with Colonel Eastland until he regained his health.

Colonel Eastland had a daughter, Martha. During George's period of recuperation, he and Martha fell in love. He persuaded her to be his wife and to accompany him back North. He brought this new bride from the warmth of the South across the ice of Lake Erie in January, 1848, to live on Kelleys Island.

In the year of 1835, Addison Kelley built a large log house on the west side of Division Street, about fifteen hundred feet from the south shore of Lake Erie. This log house was not for himself, but for his father, Datus. By the time George Kelley arrived with his new bride, Datus had moved elsewhere, and so George and Martha lived in the log house. This log house forms the core of the oldest house now standing on Kelleys Island.

In August of 1849, Martha gave birth to the first twins born on the island. Unfortunately they lived only a few weeks. They had other children, one daughter in particular named Hattie. She married Mr. Stewart Chisholm of Cleveland, Ohio, and they resided in Cleveland. As Hattie was gifted with an excellent soprano voice, she sang for many years in the choir of the Second Baptist Church of Cleveland. This was the church to which Mr. John D. Rockefeller belonged. Cleveland critics judged her voice to be equal to the best soprano of the world at that time.

George Kelley made many contributions to Kelleys Island's history. He was the first postmaster. He was the first to register ear marks for hogs and cattle in the township record book. The record reads: "Irad and George Kelley left for record July 1848, round hole through the right ear." As livestock wandered the island, these ear marks served as identification in case a dispute arose over the proper ownership of an animal.

George also operated a general store. In 1854, he traded his store business to William S. Webb in exchange for Webb's quarry. He then opened several small quarries in various places on the island. He built a dock for shipping his stone. Here the keel for the *Island Queen,* which was put into service in 1855, was laid.

George Kelley is an example of the many versatile pioneers who made Kelleys Island a growing and prosperous community.

# The Tiber River

Today a person would laugh in disbelief if anyone were to tell him that a small stream on Kelleys Island was once a river. There was a time when the water level of Lake Erie was much lower than it now is, and the south shore of Kelleys Island extended much further out into the water. The island's only stream, known as the Tiber River, ran past what is now Al Rumel's property out into Lake Erie. At the mouth of the river in 1834 there was a flat large enough to be used as a shipyard.

In the 1850s, Kelleys Island, then a township, was divided into two districts, District No. 1 and District No. 2. At a meeting of the township officers on March 1, 1852, the road supervisor of District No. 2 was authorized to construct a bridge across the Tiber River. Before this it was necessary to ford the river with teams of horses, or pedestrians could walk a small single-plank foot bridge. Today the stream is covered with a stone culvert, and the road has been filled in and built up almost fifteen feet above its former level. Sometimes there's scarcely a trickle of water running through the stream.

After the bridge was built, a drayman was attempting to cross it while driving a blind horse. In a moment of carelessness, he drove off the road into the river. The water running through was so swift that it carried driver, horse, and wagon out into the lake. The horse broke loose from the wagon and got safely to shore. The man, who wasn't able to swim, was soon swept into deep water.

Mr. John Estes (father of the donor of Kelleys Island Public School) was passing by and heard the man's cry for help. He swam to his rescue. As there was quite a current, both men nearly drowned. Others saw the commotion, found a boat nearby, and saved the two men.

Today children wade in the mouth of the Tiber River and pick up huge carp that come there to spawn. In the hot summer months when the stream is dry, no one would believe that it was once a river and a shipyard.

# A Heroic Rescue

Islanders respect a northeaster! (Contrary to the New Englanders' pronunciation, *nor'easter,* islanders pronounce the word as I've written it.) Although some very sudden southerly winds of gale force are dangerous, especially if one is in a small boat, it is the northeaster that's dreaded. This wind builds up gradually and pushes mountainous waves from a considerable distance down the lake. By the time these waves reach the island, they have gained a powerful momentum. The water level of Lake Erie in the islands area has reached record heights during a northeast storm, causing flooding, erosion, destruction, and loss of lives.

The greatest storms of the nineteenth century occurring between 1857 and 1862 were northeasters. Probably the worst of all was in August, 1861, when the main dock at Kelleys Island was destroyed. In June of 1902 another such storm occurred. On June 28th of that year, the steamer *George Dunbar* left Cleveland, Ohio, bound for Alpena, Michigan. It carried a crew of ten people. During the night a northeaster of gale force sprang up. The *Dunbar* battled the waves of the storm until it reached just east of Kelleys Island, where it could struggle no longer. There it sank.

Five of the crew sought safety in a life raft, but they couldn't stay afloat in such a sea. All drowned. The other five, which included Captain Little, his wife and daughter, left the ship in a yawl boat which soon capsized. Two of this party also drowned. Only the captain and his family, who were using life preservers, remained afloat. As they were being carried past Kelleys Island by the waves and current, a group of people who had come to the east side of the island to watch the breakers saw them. Most of these islanders thought it impossible to attempt to rescue Captain Little and his family.

Fred Dishinger, noted then as an experienced fisherman, his grown son, Fred, Jr., and James Hamilton, who was mayor of the island at the time, found a flat bottomed skiff which they dragged to the water. In spite of such a treacherous sea, they launched the boat and ventured into the lake. Two men rowed while the other one bailed water to keep the skiff afloat until they reached those left of the shipwrecked crew. They threw a rope to Captain Little, who tied it to his preserver and then fastened it to his wife and daughter. Thus the men towed them to shore and to safety.

These three men were applauded as heroes. Each of the rescuers was awarded a gold medal by the United States Government inscribed with his name and this statement: "For heroic daring in saving life, June 29, 1902."

## The Fate of Five Quarrymen

During the early 1900s, many foreign people who could speak no English settled on Kelleys Island. They came to work in the quarries or vineyards. Near the northwestern part of the island several Italian, Sicilian, and Slovak families lived almost unto themselves, as if they weren't really a part of the other inhabitants of the island, in what was known as "lime company houses." For various reasons many of these people changed their family names. Some shortened their names; others changed them completely. Because of these changes and the life-styles of these people, the older island settlers were not well enough acquainted with them to identify them easily.

In 1911, on Saturday, September 23rd, about 1:00 o'clock p.m., a nude body washed ashore on the north shore of Kelleys Island. The legs of the body were tightly strapped together between the knees and the thighs, and there was a rope about ten feet in length tied around the waist. There was a deep gash on the right side of the face, extending from the ear to below the chin. The body was described as that of a man five feet, four inches in height, weighing about one hundred sixty pounds, about thirty-five years old, with short black hair and a clean-shaven face. At first no one could identify the body. Several foreigners who worked in the quarry had found the body, and they assumed that the man had been murdered and thrown overboard from a vessel.

On Monday, September 25th, Deputy Coroner John Casey of Sandusky, Ohio, identified the body as that of Antonio Dicarie. This man was not some stranger thrown overboard from a vessel, but he was a Sicilian who worked in the quarry on the island. Islanders told a reporter from the *Sandusky Register* that he shared a lime company house with four other men whom they named as John Barlana, Rothe Klowetch, Dominico Silwate, and Antonio Berlin. These four men were not available for questioning. Deputy Casey was told that Barlana and Klawetch had left the island the Thursday before on the steamer *Kirby* without drawing their pay, and that the other two men had left Friday on either the *Kirby* or the *Arrow*. He learned also that Dicarie had worked all day on Tuesday, September 19th, but when he did not come to work on Wednesday, the quarry's foreman was told that Dicarie was ill.

Deputy Casey went to the house where the men lived. There he found an upstairs room splattered with blood, a bed covered with blood, and splotches of blood leading to the lake, but no one was at home. On the next day, Tuesday, September 26th, the island's marshal, Henry Elfers, Jr., found clothing belonging to the murdered man secreted upon a ledge in the cellar, shoved up under the foundation of the house.

Stories were circulating around the island that these five men had quarreled over paying their share of living expenses. It looked, indeed, as if the four men might have murdered their housemate, and that their motive was revenge and robbery. Money known to belong to Dicarie was missing.

On Friday, September 29th, Albert Erne, an island fisherman, discovered two more bodies that had been shot and stabbed several times, weighted down with rocks, on the north shore near where Dicarie's body had been found. These men were identified as Antonio Berlin and Jim Berlin, previously named by islanders as John Barlana. Whoever reported that Berlin and Barlana had left the island were mistaken. They had without doubt been murdered at the same time that Dicarie was.

Deputy Casey began immediately to trace the whereabouts

of Klowetch and the other man whose name was given as Dominico Silwate, Seldaggio, and Silvage. Whether this was a misspelling, a case of mistaken identity, or a case where there was a change of a family name, I do not know. The deputy soon learned that they had left the island on Thursday or Friday with trunks and other baggage. They had spent Friday night at Marblehead, Ohio, with Paul Ruffa, a cousin of the Berlins. At the railroad station they had checked a trunk to Cleveland, Ohio, and had inquired about train connections to Sharon and Pittsburgh, Pennsylvania.

Klowetch had dark piercing eyes and a habit of casting quick and suspicious glances. This characteristic, along with the thoroughness of Deputy Casey, led authorities to the murderers. On October 1, 1911, the two men were apprehended at an Italian rooming house in Pittsburgh. In their possession was $514.00 in money, $94.00 of it in silver, a revolver, and a hat covered with blood.

These men were arrested for murder. They stood trial, were found guilty, and were executed in the Ohio Penitentiary. Some say that the bodies of all five men, the murdered and the murderers, lie side-by-side in unmarked graves in Kelleys Island's cemetery. I have no facts to substantiate this. We do know that they did not return to Sicily or Italy as they had originally planned to do.

# A Snowstorm Tragedy

At one time when winter enclosed Kelleys Island, residents risked rough seas or thin ice to get to the mainland. Not so today. Airplane taxis, which have become popular during summer as well as winter months, supply the necessary transportation. A few years ago islanders worked together to make a municipal airport with lighted runways extending both east-west and north-south. With this facility, planes can land both day and night.

At one time at least four or more airlines served Kelleys Island. One of these, Sky Tours, Inc., worked out of Sandusky, Ohio, in the 1960s. In 1963 the company moved to Port Clinton where it became Island Air Lines.

Unseasonably warm weather and wind prevailed in January of 1962. On February 2nd of that year, snow began falling, and by late evening a blinding storm had developed. In spite of such weather, four young people, Carol Perruchon, a native of Kelleys Island, Dolores Pilney, her brother Bruce, and Carol Cline, all of Cleveland, Ohio, asked Sky Tours, Inc., to charter them from Sandusky to Kelleys Island. They were planning to spend the weekend at a rented apartment on the island.

The pilot on duty that evening was Chester Dietrick, and he agreed to fly these people to Kelleys Island. As the single engine Cessna used by Sky Tours couldn't accommodate four passengers at one time, Chester agreed to make two trips. The snow had stopped falling when he took off with his first two passengers, Carol Perruchon and Bruce Pilney. They landed safely sometime between 7:00 and 7:30 p.m., and the pilot returned for the other two girls.

As it suddenly began snowing again, those waiting at the Kelleys Island airport to pick up these passengers were at first unconcerned when the plane didn't return within the usual time it takes to make the trip over and back, about a half hour. However, when two hours had elapsed, people began to be concerned. They tried to call the Sandusky airport by phone but could get no answer. Fearing that the pilot might have missed the runway, a search party was formed. For most of the night islanders searched the woods and quarries, to no avail.

In the meantime, around 11:45 p.m., the island's constable notified Erie County's Sheriff Department that the plane due to arrive on Kelleys Island hadn't landed. A deputy sheriff then notified Ralph Dietrick, uncle of the pilot and also manager of Sky Tours. He and a deputy rushed to the airport where they discovered that the plane, passengers, and pilot in question were gone. Immediately an alert was broadcast across the state and country in case the pilot had attempted a landing elsewhere. Civil defense, police and air bands picked up the alert.

The morning of February 3rd was a gray, misty morning. Visibility was very low. However, Sky Tours sent out a search plane to circle an area around Sandusky and Kelleys Island. Soon, about six miles east of Kelleys, the shattered wreckage was found. On an ice floe lay a demolished airplane and two bodies.

Because of the mist, the condition of the ice, and open water, attempting a rescue was difficult. Helicopters were dispatched to the scene by the Ohio State Patrol and the Navy at Grosse Ile, Michigan. At ten o'clock a.m. the Ohio Patrol copter's pilot, Joseph Szabo, and co-pilot, James E. Haines, landed about one thousand feet from open water. They confirmed three deaths, two girls, Dolores Pilney and Carol Cline, outside the aircraft, and the pilot, Chester Dietrick, still strapped in his seat.

## The Disappearance of Elizabeth Selfe

The Selfe family, Mr. Selfe, his wife Elizabeth, and their children migrated from England to Pelee Island in Canada during the 1800s. However, they were disillusioned with life as they found it on Pelee. Hearing of prosperity derived from quarrying and other activities, the Selfes moved on to Kelleys Island. They arrived in a sailboat with all their worldly possessions.

There was a vacant house belonging to Herman Koster located next to St. Michael's Church. For a short while this place was a home for the Selfes. Mr. Selfe sought work in one of the quarries to provide for his family.

Not long after their arrival, Mr. Selfe became ill. The nature of this illness isn't recorded, but it proved to be fatal. His family was left in dire circumstances. Many islanders came to their aid. A house on Mr. Robert Hamilton's property located on the lower part of Long Point was given to them rent free. As it was a wooded area, it was a rather lonely place for this young widow and her children, but it served as a comfortable home for a few years.

During the night of June 27, 1877, Mrs. Selfe disappeared. When her children, Jennie, who was then aged ten, and James, age of fourteen years, reported her absence, many islanders helped in an island-wide search for her. For several days the search continued, but they could find no trace of the missing woman.

On June 31, 1877, the editor of the *Sandusky Register* interviewed Jennie and James Selfe to see if they could furnish any clues to their mother's whereabouts. When questioned, Jennie replied as follows: "Mother got our supper at about seven o'clock; complained of a pain in the head; ate a hearty supper; after supper, in doing up the work, said she didn't know what she was about; never said such a thing before; all went to bed at about 9:00; thought I saw a man looking in the window; was then in bed; he had on a dark hat turned up; his face was close to the glass.

"Mother got up, wrapped a quilt around herself, and went and looked and shut down the window blind; then came back and sat down by me and said I must have been mistaken. I slept a long time after that, then heard mother get out of bed and scream; ran around the room and kept on screaming. She then lay down on the floor between my bed and the other one and quit screaming; kept striking the floor with her feet on screaming constantly; did not ask her what was the matter until she quit, then she only said, or muttered, 'Ugh, ugh.' Reached up and turned down the lamp until it went out; then I saw her creep out (the moon was shining) of our room into the other. I know it was Mother that put out the light.

"I thought I heard her walk around in the other room about five minutes. Then I heard the door open and shut and heard no more noise. If there had been any man in our room when she was in it I could have seen him. She had a quilt wrapped around her while walking around the room." The editor reported that these were the statements of the girl substantially in her own words and almost literally.

Next James told his story to the newspaper editor: "I heard

my mother say two or three times, while washing clothes that she did not know what was about. I saw no one at the window. Heard Mother screaming on the floor. She screamed about five minutes. Was lying on a quilt. Quit screaming and reached up her hand and put out the lamp. I knew it was she who put out the light. Then saw her in a leaning posture going into the other room. While out there heard the cupboard door open. Then I suppose Mother went out. I was alarmed when I heard her screaming."

On this date the editor concluded that if there was any violence, it appeared almost conclusively that it must have been after she went out of the house.

On July 9th, 1877, a story appeared in the *Sandusky Register* reporting that the body of Mrs. Selfe was found in the lake east of Dwelle's residence at Kelleys Island on Saturday. According to this story, Erie County Coroner Stanley had been notified.

As there were marks on the woman's body, especially around her face and neck, islanders suspected she had been murdered. There was much speculation as to how the death had occurred, and many rumors circulated concerning the woman. People were dissatisfied with Justice of the Peace Howlett's inquest and expressed a desire for a second inquest. Some jurors refused to sign the verdict. They were even willing to defray a part of or all, if necessary, expenses incurred. Many thought there was an island man involved, and some even went so far as to name him. However, he was not apprehended or questioned by authorities, and a second inquest was refused. No one ever learned if Mrs. Selfe died by accident, committed suicide, or was murdered by a mysterious stanger or maybe a fellow islander.

## Lost at Sea

Even though cemeteries are sad places to visit, they're interesting. They record births and deaths, and in many cases where graves of families lie in one plot of ground, they record family histories. Kelleys Island's cemetery is located on Division Street, probably a half-mile south of Glacial Grooves. It was begun in 1854. Prior to that date, burials were made in private burial places. There are stones in the cemetery showing dates of death before 1854. Although I have no accurate knowledge concerning these dates, I wonder if bodies of the deceased could have been placed elsewhere and later transferred to the main cemetery.

There is one white marble stone near the northeast corner of the cemetery bearing the following inscription: John McDonald—Died Jan. 11, 1854 Aged 26 Yrs. John was the man who first prepared the plot of ground for burial purposes. According to the record, he was not doing an adequate job and was taken to task for his carelessness. He replied that he didn't care how the work was done as he didn't expect to be buried there. John was also working in Mr. William Webb's quarry, and on January 11, 1854, he was accidentally killed. As fate would have it, he was the first to be buried in the Kelleys Island Cemetery.

In about the center of the cemetery there are two other stones, not side-by-side, but each bearing the figure of a boy shouldering a gun with a dog alongside the boy. These stones are inscribed as follows: Son—Jackie Betzenheimer 1941-1958 and Son-Richard Bugel 1938-1958. My heart is heavy as I look at these two graves, because I knew these boys well, and I feel that their deaths were so tragic. Both Jackie and Dick (our nickname for Richard) were pupils in my high school English classes. Dick was graduated in 1956; Jackie was a senior at the time of his death.

One classroom experience comes to mind as I remember Jackie. We were studying *Macbeth,* and this was his first introduction to Shakespeare. As he was very outspoken, he told me that he wasn't at all interested in *Macbeth,* and he thought

53

The Kelleys Island cemetery where John McDonald was the first man to prepare a plot of ground for burial purposes, and, though he didn't expect to be, was the first person to be buried there.

his dad, an island commercial fisherman, would be ashamed of him if he should go home talking like Shakespeare. I explained that the poet's English was, indeed, a foreign language in comparison to ours, and I agreed to translate as best I could into our vernacular as we read. Well, we lived with Macbeth for several days and then went on to something else. Six-weeks' test time came around, and as I observed Jackie struggling with his test, I noticed that he seemed to be having problems. "Is anything wrong?" I asked him. With a smirk on his face he answered, "Will you tell me why I can't remember anything except that darn fool Macbeth? He was a real character." Jackie's mastery of *Macbeth* didn't do him much good. Maybe if we had taught some life-saving techniques, the tragedy wouldn't have happened.

Another incident concerning Jackie seems more appropriate in memory of the Jackie we knew. At the time he was a young boy and our neighbor. Often when he went to school or to the downtown area, he crossed through our backyard and through the fields instead of using the conventional sidewalks, usually with his dog, Susie, following.

Our cocker spaniel, Lady, had given birth to some puppies. When Jackie stopped at our house with his dad to see them, he reached into the dog's bed to pick up one of them and the mother snapped at him. From then on, we knew when Jackie was passing by, as Lady barked ferociously. She would not let him come near the house unless we commanded her to be quiet. He understood because of his love and concern for animals.

Jackie lived for hunting season. He often awoke long before daylight, took his gun and Susie, and headed for the lakeshore on the east side of the island where wild mallards congregated. He hunted until time for school when he'd park his gun somewhere and send the dog home. On Saturday morning, December 7, 1958, Jackie, Dick Bugel, and Mike McCune went to the east side of the island to see how many mallards they could bag. According to Mike, an enormously large flock of ducks settled on the water, too far away for them to shoot. An old canoe was lying on the beach. Jackie and Dick grabbed it and the oars and paddled out to the flock. The ducks were so thick that the boys went right in among them and hit some on the head with their oars. They were having so much fun that they became careless, and their canoe overturned.

Both were wearing heavy hunting clothes and boots. Instead of staying with the canoe, they tried to swim ashore. The weight of their clothes and the icy water wouldn't let them make much headway. Mike ran for help, but it came too late. Both boys drowned. Although for several days islanders dragged the lake trying to recover their bodies, it was late in December when Jackie was found. The next spring Dick's body floated to the top of the water down the lake near Huron, Ohio. The losing of two young lives so quickly was a tragedy that all islanders mourned for many months.

There is another spot in the cemetery where Gilbert A. Riedy, 1909-1952, and Son Edwin J., 1947-1952, are buried. Gilbert, better known to his acquaintances as "Mike," was an islander and a seafaring man. In 1939 he had a boat built on Kelleys Island to his specifications; he christened it the *Rene Dene*. Along with his brother Eugene and another boat named *The Pal*, Mike did some gillnetting and took out fishing parties on Lake Erie. In this way he earned a living to support his wife and a family of four children.

In the summer of 1946, one evening Mike invited several people to go aboard the *Rene Dene* and out into the lake to try their luck with hook and line. He started the engine, untied the lines, and was hardly away from the dock when the engine blew, sending several aboard the boat into the lake. One of the passengers, "Jake" Martin, who was badly burned, swam back to a dock nearby, started his own boat, and went to the *Rene Dene* to rescue those aboard. Later in the evening he and some of the other passengers had to be transported to a hospital in Sandusky for treatment for severe burns. Fortunately, at this time no lives were lost.

After a time the *Rene Dene* was repaired and put back into service. Five years later, in October of 1952, one morning Mike and his five-year-old son, Eddie, put some cargo aboard the boat and headed for Sandusky. Mike's brother Eugene and the same friend who had rescued the passengers in 1946 were watching from the shore. They saw Mike and Eddie nearing the Marblehead lighthouse. Suddenly they heard an explosion and saw fire and debris fly into the air. As soon as they could, they manned another boat and headed toward the *Rene Dene*. They circled it, but because of fire and floating debris, they couldn't get near it. They saw neither of the occupants. Several days later a fisherman found Mike's body a short distance off Kelleys Island. Not long afterward, his son Eddie's body was recovered from the depths of Lake Erie. The *Rene Dene* was never recovered.

## Tom Jones

Many corners of the world have a Tom Jones. He might be a fictional character, a well-known singer, or a common laborer who fits into some niche of community life. Kelleys Island had its own Tom Jones, Thomas Hoyt Jones, Jr., a financier also of Bratenahl, Ohio.

In the late 1930s, the Jones family bought property referred to as Long Point on the northeastern point of the island. Tom and his brother Brooks were young boys then. Their father was the Jones of Jones, Day, Reavis & Pogue, one of the largest law firms in Cleveland. When Mr. Jones passed away, he was cremated and his ashes were placed in a hole of a large stone on the property overlooking Lake Erie.

Young Brooks married a woman, from whom he was later divorced, who was to become Mrs. Cyrus Eaton. The two had one daughter. Sometime after his divorce, he remarried and had a son, Tom.

Thomas Hoyt Jones, a fighter pilot in World War II, married Virginia Hosford, and they had two sons, Tim and Mark. After Mark had grown to adulthood, Tom and Virginia divorced, and she remarried. He never did.

Tragedy seemed to stalk Tom's life. He loved boating, and the rougher the water the more it challenged him. Once he had his wife, their sons, and her children by a former marriage out on the water. Not taking all of the moods of Lake Erie into consideration, he plowed his fast boat onto land, sending his wife and children to a hospital. When his son Tim was approaching adolescence, he was killed while riding his bicycle near his home. His former wife died in her sleep in a hotel in Munich. After Tom's death, their son Mark was killed in an automobile accident.

The Jones families spent many months of each year on Kelleys Island. Every resident knew Tom, an extremely friendly person. He seldom came to the commercial part of the island ("up-town") unless he wore a navy blazer, open shirt, an ascot, sunglasses, and his captain's hat, and his golden retriever was by his side. He often walked into my kitchen and helped himself to a banana or to green onions, fresh from our garden, which he dipped in salt before eating. In later years he came with his servant Moses Strowder, who looked after him like a mother hen.

In the last few years of his life Tom brought other servants to the island, all young black men from Cleveland. In the late summer of 1984, he brought Angelo, also known as Darnell Vaughn, a part-time employee, with him. Vaughn was a black male of light complexion, black medium-length hair, brown eyes, five feet, six inches tall, and weighed about one hundred and fifteen pounds. But Moses was still his loyal and faithful servant.

One Sunday afternoon in November of 1984, Tom flew to the island, bringing Vaughn with him, supposedly to close his cottage for the winter. Between six and seven o'clock on Monday evening of November 5th, the island's police chief, Charles Moore, received a telephone call from Moses Strowder asking him to check the Jones' cottage to see if everything was all right. Tom was to have returned to Cleveland; he hadn't done so, and there was no answer to the phone. When the police chief reached the cottage, he found Tom's body in the bathroom. The golden retriever was there, but Vaughn was gone along with Jones' 1983 Dodge Aries station wagon, which had left the island on the 9:00 a.m. ferry to Marblehead.

A warrant was issued for Vaughn's arrest, at first for theft of the station wagon and then for questioning about the death, which was ruled a homicide. Vaughn telephoned Cleveland police and surrendered to them on November 12th as he sat in the Dodge Aries. He was extradited to Erie County and held in jail there on a $50,000 bond. Then during the week of November 12th, Vaughn was charged with murder. Jones had died of strangulation according to Erie County and Cuyahoga County coroners' offices. Vaughn confessed to the murder as well as to the thefts of the car and some other items such as a watch and a television set. He claimed that he killed in self-defense while trying to ward off a sexual attack by Jones. Even though a jury was sympathetic to Vaughn's situation, they found him guilty of auto theft and murder. He was sentenced to fifteen years in prison at the Lima Correctional Facility, a medium security prison.

On August 21, 1985, Vaughn attempted an escape. He had been working in a box factory of the prison but was missing when a head count was made. Later that evening he was found hiding in a box. He was placed in solitary confinement and later transferred to Lucasville, a maximum security prison.

Those of us who knew Tom Jones miss him. He was a part of the island community. When a small piece of that is gone, bigger "chunks" soon follow, and everything changes, not always for the better.

## Carrying the Mail

Of all the islands' tales, those told by the winter mail carriers are some of the most fascinating. Though all the carriers have had many similar experiences, each has at least one unique story to tell, some humorous and some quite tragic.

Almost every trip for carrying the winter mail was an adventure because of heavy ice, thin ice, running ice, rough ice, miles of ice piling, icebergs, no ice at all, heavy snow, blinding snow, fog, and strange noises to mislead the carrier and cause him to go astray. Running ice was the most threatening of all, because it goes faster than a man can walk. If his boat were caught in it, it took all the strength and ingenuity he had to keep from going down the lake with the ice.

For these adventures, the carrier used a vessel called an "Iron Clad." This was a flat bottomed boat about fourteen or sixteen feet long. On the bottom there were two runners, usually made of oak shod with iron, so that the boat could be used as a sled on ice. There was a sail on the bow to carry the boat through the water or over ice when conditions called for such. The sides of the boat were sheathed with galvanized iron, thus the name, because thin ice is very powerful and can cut through wood like a sharp knife. Each boat was equipped with oars for use when necessary as well as strong ropes for pulling the boat.

The men who were brave enough to assume such a task during the cold winter months had to be dressed for the job. Besides warm clothing, they wore hip boots to which an extra sole of leather was added. Bradded steel plates were attached to the sole by a blacksmith, and it was said that the men could walk up the side of an iceberg with these boots. Sometimes pulling the iron clad became such a strenuous task that the men shed all their clothing down to their trousers and boots.

In addition to carrying the mail, the men often took passengers along, for which service a fee, usually one dollar, was charged. As there was no boat or plane services in those days, crossing the ice on foot was the only way to get to the mainland and back. To be assured of a fairly safe journey and for companionship, the patron was willing to pay his fee, even if it meant just walking along beside the boat. He, too, would be warmly dressed, wearing what is known as a pair of "creepers" attached to his boots or shoes in order to navigate on ice.

Henry Elfers of Kelleys Island was known as "Veteran Mail Carrier of the Islands." He held this position for over forty years, during which time he had many interesting adventures. Once he was on the ice with a cutter when the ice broke up. His horse was brought to shore in a rowboat. During the winter of 1896, he and his son were on their way to Kelleys Island from Marblehead. They were a half mile from the island when they were caught in a blizzard with the temperature below zero. He said that the snow was so blinding that he could not see his son at the end of their sixteen-foot boat. They couldn't come ashore at Kelleys because ice had piled up against the bank. They fought their way against the elements to return to Marblehead, which they reached four hours later.

During the late 1800s, the Hitchcock family carried the mail for the Bass Islands. In December of 1898, Captain Amos Hitchcock ran into thin ice while carrying the mail between North Bass and Middle Bass Islands. Strapping the bag of mail to his back, he lay down on the ice and crawled over a mile to Middle Bass. At another time, on his way from Port Clinton in a horse drawn sleigh carrying some passengers and several

*The arrival of the mail boat and passengers on the south shore of Kelleys Island on a cold winter's day.*

hundred pounds of mail, he found a crack in the ice that was too wide to jump. Not willing to give in to such adverse circumstances, he cut a large cake of ice big enough to hold his horse, sleigh, and cargo, and ferried everything across the crack to safe ice.

In the winter of 1897 and '98, the Hitchcock brothers, while carrying the mail, were caught in a storm and running ice. They were carried down the lake for some distance and were feared to be lost. Concerned islanders sent a telegram to Kelleys Island which read, "Look out for the carriers; they are fast in the ice and drifting that way." However, the men escaped from the drift and did reach shore. They were exhausted and completely covered with ice. Their caps were frozen fast to their heads and their clothes so weighty that they couldn't bend. In the process of changing clothes, they shed a bushel of ice which was swept from the floor.

George Morrison and his brother-in-law, Carl Rotert, were carrying the mail between Catawba Island and South Bass in the winter of 1903. There was a large heavy piece of metal in their boat. While maneuvering over the ice, the metal shifted, causing the boat to capsize and throwing the two men into open water. Morrison managed to climb out of the water onto safer ice, but Rotert was swept away under the ice, and Morrison was unable to save him. After the break-up of the ice in the spring, his body was found floating.

Fred Ouelette, along with his son Henry Ouelette and Henry Amonite, was carrying the mail for Pelee Island from the island to Point Pelee on the mainland during the winter of 1919-1920. On one return trip from Point Pelee, Jack Lidwell and Henry Stewart were passengers. They had left about 1:00 p.m. on Monday and soon ran into extremely dense fog. They couldn't see land anywhere and didn't know which way to go as their compass wasn't functioning properly. When darkness came upon them, they decided it would be wise to stop where they were and wait for daylight. By morning the fog was still thick. Henry Amonite thought he heard a rooster crow and started off alone, as he couldn't persuade the others to follow him. Finally, the four other men decided they were going in the right direction. Meanwhile, as the men had not come home by noon on Tuesday, a cablegram was sent to Leamington that the mailmen and passengers were lost. The Heinz Factory whistle and the Water Works whistle began to sound an alarm. Four miles away on frozen Lake Erie the men heard this. They followed the sound and by 4:30 p.m. they reached shore. Henry Amonite had arrived at 10:00 a.m., as the rooster he heard was a real one, and its crowing led him in the right direction.

On a very cold, clear day in January of 1921, Guy McCormick, his son Harry, and Ray Hooper carried the mail across the ice to Point Pelee with intentions of returning to Pelee Island after they'd eaten lunch. Two passengers, Verne Kiff and Andy Graham, wanted to accompany them on the return trip. Guy tried to persuade Andy that he shouldn't try the crossing. Andy, who weighed at least three hundred pounds, was fearful of the lake, but he was concerned about a fishery that he owned at Pelee Island.

Andy sat in the afterpart of the Iron Clad as it moved over frozen Lake Erie. The men hadn't gone far when they ran into thin ice. As the boat kept breaking through because of the weight it was carrying, Guy said, "Andy, you will have to get out and walk. We cannot carry you."

Andy got out of the boat, took about three steps, and down through the ice he went. The men pulled him out, put him back into the boat, and tried to make some headway. It took all everyone could do to keep the boat moving, and they ignored Andy for awhile. Soon Harry McCormick called to Guy, "Dad, come back here and look at this man. I think he has passed out. He hasn't moved a muscle." Guy had the men help him to lift Andy up. When Roy tried to open his eyelid, he said, "He's dead." The men proceeded to Pelee Island. The next day the same men returned the corpse back across the same ice to Point Pelee.

# More Winter Tales

In addition to tales told about the islands' mail carriers, there are other adventures worth recording, most of which concern winter weather. In 1912 a funeral procession with casket and mourners on bobsleds went from Sandusky, Ohio, to Kelleys Island across a frozen lake. A few years later an entire funeral procession drove across the ice from Sandusky to Kelleys Island in automobiles.

During extremely cold winters if the ice is good, driving on ice is an everyday happening. An adventuresome individual will test the ice, and as he goes he marks a trail with various objects such as cedar branches or brush. If his path is safe, then he can return via the same route and soon others will follow. Many safe crossings are made in open cars. Ice fishermen often drive to their good fishing spots. In 1936 one hundred eighty automobiles crossed from Marblehead to Kelleys Island in one day without mishap.

Henry "Heinie" Elfers and Charles A. Himmelein operated the Kelleys Island Transportation Company which took passengers and freight across the ice from Kelleys Island to Sandusky. For this service they used two horses, Dick and Billy, and a sleigh. On February 24th, 1912, the two men left the island for Sandusky with seven passengers and freight. They went through the ice but managed to save everything except for two barrels of wine. Landing the passengers at Marblehead, Elfers and Himmelein left for Sandusky but didn't get far before their horses again went through the ice. For a second time they were able to rescue Dick and Billy. However, when they left Sandusky for the return trip home, they were about a half mile from Bay Point near Marblehead when for the third time the team went through, taking the sled, two passengers, and all of the freight with them. Heinie swam to the horses. He tried to free them by cutting off their harness, but it seemed that the poor animals were doomed. His efforts failed, and both horses died, either from exhaustion or strangulation. The men walked back to Sandusky.

The next day, taking some help with them, they went to the spot where they had lost their horses and recovered part of the freight: some twine, two barrels of beer, some oysters, and some lard. They were also able to bring their bobsled to surface.

A seventeen year old girl from Cleveland, Ruth Silburg, was one of the passengers. "I can't recall what I did when the sled went through the ice," she told a reporter. "I guess I must have clung to the ice, or the sled or something or other, until Mr. Himmelein dived in and pulled me out. I do know I would undoubtedly have drowned but for him."

There have been winters when the lake was only partially frozen, and steamers would butt their way through heavy ice floes to get to Marblehead or Sandusky from Kelleys Island. For several years the ice breaker, *American Eagle,* kept the lake open after navigation season had closed for the winter. A steamer named the *Lakeside* took its place.

One winter day when ice was unusually thick the *Lakeside* left Sandusky with nearly a hundred passengers on board. Plans were to pick up a herd of beef cattle at Marblehead and then proceed to Kelleys Island. The passage leading into Sandusky Bay was open, but around Marblehead ice was almost two feet thick, and it was difficult to make any headway. The steamer would back up and go forward, striking a tremendous blow with its steel hull to the solid ice sheet until it broke into huge blocks. The *Lakeside's* captain asked the passengers to go to the stern of the boat so that the bow would rise. The steamer was then driven full speed ahead up onto the ice. Passengers would then run forward to the bow, and their weight caused the ice to yield. For two hours they played this game until they arrived safely at the Marblehead dock.

In 1904, the *Lakeside* became the *Olcott.* She was rechristened when her owners had her cut in two, and a thirty-foot section was built into her amidship. On a December day in 1910, many islanders boarded the *Olcott* at Kelleys Island to travel to Sandusky. There was ice at the mouth of the channel of Sandusky Bay. Here the *Olcott's* condenser intake pipes became clogged with ice, and the steamer could go no further.

She was stuck. Around 6:00 o'clock p.m., some of the male passengers left the boat; around 10:00 p.m., the United States Government life-saving crew from Marblehead took four women who were aboard the boat into Sandusky. Those who remained on the steamer had only fish to eat, and these were taken from a barrel that had been shipped as freight. Evidently the *Olcott* was freed, though history doesn't say how or when, because in 1917 she was sold to European allies and was taken to salt water via the St. Lawrence River.

On Thursday, November 3rd, 1898, a small twenty-four foot boat named the *J.Q.* had arrived in Kingsville, Ontario from Pelee Island. Those on board were the skipper, Hugh Hooper, Fred White, and the owner of the boat, Charles Barnes. Mr. Hooper had brought some potatoes which he had grown on Pelee to sell in Kingsville. He was eager to return home with the money as well as winter supplies, because he had left his wife Mildred as well as two small sons, Roy and Byrd, on the island. Two of his sisters, May and Victoria, planned to return with him. By Sunday, November 6th, he and the others had completed their business and were ready to go home.

The mail boat, the *Ravenna,* was leaving for Pelee, and as there was a gale blowing, Mr. Hooper decided to follow the mail boat. The men on the *Ravenna* tried to persuade him to wait for calmer weather, but Mr. Hooper was determined to go. His two sisters refused an invitation to transfer from it to the mail boat, expressing confidence in the *J.Q.*

Both boats plowed through giant waves until they were about three or four miles from Pelee. Suddenly the *J.Q.* disappeared from sight of the *Ravenna's* captain. Although the *Ravenna* began to take on water, the men aboard bailed and they made it into McCormick's dock.

Residents of Pelee scanned Lake Erie with binoculars and walked the beaches, hoping to find some remnants of the *J.Q.'s* passengers. On the following Monday, the *J.Q.* with the body of Charles Barnes lashed to it came ashore. Seemingly he hadn't drowned, because he had removed his outer clothing, and his suspenders were tied as though he had tried to secure someone else to him. The other bodies weren't recovered until spring. Lake Erie had again won a battle.

In February of 1886, an ice breaker previously mentioned, the *American Eagle,* captained by F.J. Magle, left Carpenter's Point on Kelleys Island for Middle Bass Island at 7:00 o'clock a.m. As ice between the two islands was very thick in certain areas, the boat needed some assistance. George Gascoyne came with horse drawn ice plows and a crew of men. They cut grooves on each side of the boat and holes every hundred feet or so just enough to weaken the ice. Captain Magle would back up the vessel, speed ahead, and break the ice. He reached Middle Bass at 4:00 o'clock p.m., having covered a distance of about six miles.

The Bass Islands haven't escaped tragedies of Lake Erie's treacherous ice. In February 1923, Dr. Theodore C. Griest and his nurse, Sylvia Schultz, were testing the ice in an automobile the evening before their planned trip from Put-in-Bay to the mainland. They fell through an open hole about fifty feet in diameter west of Green Island. A search party of islanders recovered the body of Ms. Schultz and pulled up the car. The next day the body of Dr. Griest was found.

Dr. George J. Edam had come to serve the Bass Islands in November, 1939. The following February he was giving his wife and two children a ride on the ice when their automobile went through thin ice near Middle Bass. Middle Bass's postmistress, Mildred McCann, saw the car disappear and summoned help. Several citizens responded, but efforts to revive the doctor and his wife failed. The children drowned also.

Islanders Thelma and Charles Schneider and Jean and John Klacik were returning to their home on Middle Bass from a firemen's party at Put-in-Bay in 1955. Charles Schneider and Richard Bretz were following them in a second car. When only about one hundred feet from shore, the first car broke through the ice. Thelma and Jean escaped with the help of Charles Jr. and Richard. The other two men were unable to get out of the car and unfortunately lost their lives.

Many islanders used open cars, cars with their tops cut off, Model Ts and Model A Fords for ice transportation. Passengers could usually escape from these if a car broke through ice. Many cars went to the bottom of Lake Erie, only to be recovered with ropes and hoists. Others stayed on the bottom.

Although these have been tales of tragedy, sadness, ill fortune, and hard work, I'm sure there are more that can be told of fun and enjoyment which a frozen lake can provide for islanders. In addition to ice fishing and enormous catches of perch and walleye, people experience skating, ice-sailing, and in more recent years, snowmobiling. They travel back and forth between islands and from islands to the mainland for an escape from isolation and for socializing with someone besides their neighbor. However, very few of these tales are mentioned in newspapers or recorded for future generations, and only those involved know what fun they've had.

In her *Sketches and Stories of the Lake Erie Islands,* Lydia J. Ryall tells of an interesting crossing of a party of five people from Catawba Island to Leamington, Ontario, Canada, by automobile: J.P. Cagney, John Darr, Captain Wallace Smith, L.B. DeWitt, and J.C. West. They left Catawba Island for Put-in-Bay, then to North Bass, and next to Pelee Island. Here Dr. O.B. Van Epps joined them.

As they journeyed on to Leamington, there were several cracks in the ice which they literally "flew" over. Ms. Ryall wrote, "two men were placed on each side of the opening, so as to give assistance if needed. Then, backing the machine about fifty feet, the driver sent it forward at topmost speed, clearing the crack at a flying leap."

Leamington had been alerted that the group was on its way. Reporters and townspeople were watching and waiting for them, concerned for their safety. When nearly there, they came to an ice crack ten or twelve feet wide which they couldn't cross. They followed alongside it until they reached a point where they found a bridge across the open water made of sixteen-foot lengths of heavy boards. This bridge had been made previously because a man from Pelee Island was driving a sled load of tobacco from Pelee to Leamington and arrived at the crack just as a load of lumber on its way from Leamington to Pelee arrived. Some of the lumber was used for the bridge which enabled the party from Catawba to reach its destination safely. After spending a night in a hotel, they re-crossed the next day. In spite of a heavy snowstorm, they arrived back at their starting point with a record of being the first to cross the expanse of ice between the mainland of the United States and Canada in that particular area, at least, by automobile.

# THE BASS ISLANDS

The Bass Islands were named by fishermen who took home more than their share of the plentiful fish caught in the area. South Bass Island, more commonly known as Put-in-Bay, was once called Ross Island. One of the early explorers called it "Pudding Bay" because the shape of its harbor resembled a pudding bag. Long before the island was settled, Lake Erie captains knew that they could "Put-in-the-Bay" in case of storms. Whatever it has been called, it was settled somewhat later than the near-by mainland. It is made up of the Village of Put-in-Bay, which was incorporated in 1876, and the Township of Put-in-Bay. The village is centered around the bay area. The rest of South Bass in addition to North Bass, Middle Bass, and five smaller islands make up the Township. A mayor and six councilmen make up the governing body of the village; three trustees govern the township.

Around 1850, two families, the Philip Vroman and Archibold Jones families, Karl Ruh, and probably the last Indian resident lived on Put-in-Bay. It's possible that at one time many Indians lived there. Supposedly because the Indian was accused of helping himself to Ruh's maple sugar, he left the island.

Pierpont Edwards was awarded Put-in-Bay as well as Middle Bass, Sugar, Gibraltar, Ballast, and Starve Islands in order to make a straight rectangle of a land draft he had drawn in 1807 for The Connecticut Land Company.

French inhabitants lived on the island prior to the War of 1812, but there is no accurate record of how many there were.

They were driven off by Seth Dome who was an agent for the Edwards. In the summer and fall of 1811, he brought laborers to clear over a hundred acres of land on which they planted wheat. He also brought sheep and hogs. While the laborers were harvesting their wheat in the fall of 1812, British soldiers arrived, drove them from the island, and destroyed the rest of the grain.

Much has been written about Oliver Hazard Perry's victory of Lake Erie in the battle of Lake Erie, September 10th, 1813. Although this led to the end of the war, it didn't stop the fighting. It paved the way for General William Henry Harrison to accomplish that feat when he defeated the British and their Indian allies at the battle on the river Thames in October 1813. Perry used Put-in-Bay as the base of his operations, although the actual conflict between him and the British naval squadron, commanded by Commodore Robert H. Barclay, began eight miles northwest of Put-in-Bay at 11:45 A.M. and ended fourteen miles away on West Sister Island at 3:00 P.M. There the enlisted men who were killed in action were buried at sea; the officers, three Americans and three British, were brought to the shore of Put-in-Bay for burial.

Following this famous battle, Perry and Harrison planned the invasion of Canada on Put-in-Bay. More than three hundred British prisoners were taken to Port Clinton and then marched to Chillicothe, Ohio with Harrison's soldiers escorting them. By September 22nd, forty-five hundred of Harrison's soldiers were on Put-in-Bay. They moved from there to Middle Sister Island and from there to Fort Malden on September 27, 1813.

Fearing reprisals from the British, a military station existed on Put-in-Bay during much of the winter. Two hundred soldiers came from Detroit to assist the forty soldiers and twenty-three naval men already there. By spring nothing had happened to need their fighting expertise, and so they broke camp and returned to Detroit.

Although Perry's Battle of Lake Erie is the most famous one, the first blood of the War of 1812 to be shed on Ohio soil was the result of an engagement at Marblehead, Ohio. There were many Indians who were allies of the British. One hundred fifty of them confronted seventy-two American Volunteers on the

Marblehead Peninsula on September 28, 1812. U.S. soldiers were stationed at Avery, Ohio near Milan on the Huron River. Scouts who had come from Ft. Stephenson at Fremont by boat via Sandusky Bay and Cedar Point informed the soldiers of the Indians. Because of malaria and poor training, the soldiers weren't in very good condition. Nevertheless, sixty-four men volunteered to go. Eight men from Ft. Stephenson accompanied them. They sailed across Sandusky Bay, landing on the "middle orchard" near Johnson's Island. The tall grass was full of Indians who attacked from ambush. Both sides lost men. Twenty Americans took refuge in a log cabin and tried to cover the retreat of the others to the beach. However, when they reached the beach, they found no boats. The guards had taken them to Cedar Point. When they heard the gunfire, they returned with the boats and evacuated all except the twenty men in the log cabin. They lived on parched corn and roasted pumpkin until a relief force from Camp Avery rescued them several days later.

Neither side claimed victory. Eight Americans died and eight were wounded; forty Indians lost their lives. Some historians believe this skirmish tested the American strength and prevented the Indian from making a deeper penetration into nearby settlements. This could have made winning the Battle of Lake Erie more difficult.

After the War of 1812, a few settlers came to live on the island. Aschel Johnson was there for three years, then a Captain Hill and Henry and Sally Hyde. These people were representatives of a sort for A.P. Edwards. When he came in 1822, he found Ben Napier living there without permission to do so. When Edwards tried to evict Napier, the case had to be settled in Huron County Court at Norwalk, Ohio. Edwards won, and Napier went to live on Kelleys Island.

Several agents, John Pierpont, James Ross, Jacob Scott, and others began serious development of the island for Edwards. In 1823 there was a two-story summer house built for Edwards in which the agents lived. The settlers sold timber, limestone, and cordwood. Transportation to and from the mainland was supplied by the sloop *A.P. Edwards* and a large rowboat.

In the early 1830s John Pierpont built a dock in the harbor and one to the west. Unfortunately, Pierpont and two Frenchmen drowned in a sudden storm in 1836 on their way to Sandusky. Jacob Scott followed Pierpont as agent and continued with dock building and selling cordwood.

Philip Vroman, a sailor who had stopped at Put-in-Bay in 1843, became an agent for Edwards and the first permanent settler, staying for sixty-eight years. In 1854 the first physician, Luther Nelson, became an islander.

By 1852 Edwards had lost interest in his islands and wanted to sell the lot of them as one parcel. When he wasn't able to do this, he sold Green Island to the U.S. Government. In 1854 the government built a lighthouse there. He gave to his daughter, Alice, Put-in-Bay, Gibraltar, Starve, and Ballast Islands as a dowry. Her husband Elisha D. Vinton wanted cash instead of land, and so they sold their land to a Spanish merchant of New York City. By August 22, 1854, Joseph de Rivera St. Jurgo owned South Bass, Middle Bass, Sugar, Gibralter, Ballast, and Starve islands.

De Rivera began to develop the islands. Ernst Franck, the county engineer, surveyed the land into ten-acre lots and plotted roads. He put residents to work selling wood, gravel, and cedar timber and raising sheep which were shipped to New York markets.

Karl Ruh purchased a farm on the east point in 1858 and planted some grape roots, hoping to start a vineyard. Although his first efforts were disastrous, he later became a successful wine maker. Others came to try the wine business.

De Rivera's first land sale was to South Bass Island's Board of Education for one dollar. The first school was built above a hill on Catawba Avenue. Soon other land sales were made, and the real pioneers of Put-in-Bay became residents.

As was true on other Lake Erie islands, the Bass islands attracted tourists, grape growers, and wine makers. By the 1860s there were approximately five hundred people living on Put-in-Bay. A post office came into being in 1860. Put-in-Bay Township was organized, and trustees were elected in 1861. Because of agriculture on parts of the island and tourist oriented businesses on a portion of South Bass, some islanders wanted an incorporated village. They wanted to govern their own affairs. After petitioning and working out problems, they succeeded in getting the commissioners then in power to approve their petition. On June 28, 1877, the county recorder made record that Put-in-Bay was an incorporated village. The village line extended from Perry's Monument to Miller's Ferry dock, to Lakeview Avenue, on to Catawba Avenue, crossing it and Langram Rd. to the lake shore and back to the monument. It included Gibraltar Island. The rest of South Bass as well as Middle and North Bass remained a township until November 1, 1915, when a real estate development called Shore Villas was annexed to the village.

A town hall was built in 1887. A town marshal was hired in 1878, and until the town hall was built council rented part of the cellar of the Valentine Dollar building for a jail. The hall also housed the mayor's office, council room, and storage space for the fire engine. There is a large room used as an auditorium, a dance floor, a stage, and a basketball court. The hall was built on a lot donated by Valentine Dollar. The stone used in the building came from Kelleys Island.

Bodies of those who died during the early days of the island were buried near the lake's shore. Joseph de Rivera St. Jurgo donated land September 27, 1867 for the first cemetery known as Crown Hill Cemetery. As it was too small, in 1893 the village purchased land for Maple Leaf Cemetery.

The village park, a popular spot for tourists, was also given to the village by de Rivera with certain stipulations for its use and care. Later two more acres were added to the existing park land.

Put-in-Bay had no place to hold formal religious services until 1864-65. The financier, Jay Cooke who owned Gibraltar Island, and de Rivera were responsible for organizing a Protestant Episcopal religious society and donating land for a church. In the spring of 1864 the Rev. John Mills Kendrick held services in the school. In October 1865 he officiated along with R.J. Parrin, rector of Cooke's church at Chelton Hills, Pennsylvania, at the first service held in the new church.

In 1866 the Mother of Sorrows Roman Catholic Church came into being with the Reverend Mr. Charles Kueman as its pastor. This was a missionary church with St. Michaels Church on Kelleys Island as the mother. Services were held in a home until a small wood-frame church in the central part of the island was built in the 1880s. This served the congregation until 1927 when a larger church was built across from St. Paul's Episcopal Church.

Put-in-Bay hadn't experienced the benefits of modern communications until 1873 when the incorporation of the Put-in-Bay Telegraph Company came about. This company leased eight miles of wire from Western Union and maintained twenty miles of its own. Their headquarters on the island were in Idlor and Foy's store in the Doller building. The mainland station was in Sandusky. Cable came from there, across Sandusky Bay, Marblehead, and Catawba Point to Put-in-Bay. Later Hotel Victory housed one of its offices. Service was discontinued after World War II.

Telephone service came to the island in 1899. The Central Union Telephone Company was responsible for laying its first underwater telephone cable. The first three telephones on the island were used mainly to start street cars at either end of the line so that they could pass each other at Perry's Cave and for contacting the doctor's office. The switchboard was in various places at different times: Hollway's store, an alcove between the store and the town hall, and in private homes. In the 1930s dial phones replaced the hand cranked ones, and in 1973 residents were able to use direct distance dialing.

Early island residents relied on kerosene lamps and candles for lighting the dark. In time, some had their own generators. In May 1906 the Put-in-Bay Improvement Company obtained a franchise from the village council to establish an electric light system. This was expensive to operate and provided limited service. Then in 1928 the Ohio Public Service Company of Sandusky installed a flood lighting system at Perry's Monument. At first the Put-in-Bay company distributed the power. The next year an underwater cable was laid between Catawba Point and Put-in-Bay, and the Sandusky company distributed its own power. In 1950 this company merged with Ohio Edison Company which now distributes power to all of the island.

The village initiated a water and sewer system in 1904. In 1909 this was expanded, but even today not all residents can avail themselves of this village service.

As early as 1871, there were regattas held at Put-in-Bay. In

July 1884, Henry Gerlach from Cleveland was instrumental in forming the Inter-Lake Yachting Association. It was organized in January 1885. George Gardner who was mayor of Cleveland had founded the Cleveland Yachting Association. He was named first commodore of the Inter-Lake Yachting Association, I.L.Y.A., and remained so until 1893. The first regatta was held in 1885. There was a temporary lull in the I.L.Y.A.'s activities, but it reorganized in 1894, and there has been a regatta held every year since.

The state of Ohio had maintained small fish hatcheries in communities on or near Lake Erie. There was one at Kelleys Island. In 1889, the U.S. Commission of Fish and Fisheries announced that there would be a hatchery at Put-in-Bay. De Rivera sold .60 acres of land to the government on which to build it. Commercial fishermen were paid for the spawn of whitefish, herring, lake trout, pickerel, and perch. This operated until the mid 1930s.

The state built a hatchery next to the federal one in 1907. It burned but was replaced by a brick building. In 1940 the U.S. Government transferred its facilities to Ohio, and this became a research station for the Franz Theodore Stone Laboratory of Ohio State University.

There is a state park on Put-in-Bay for tent, truck, and motor home campers. It is spread over thirty-two acres. There are docks and a boat ramp. Oak Park, which is part of the park, has docks for small boats.

There are four caves which are big tourist attractions located in the center of the island. Perry's Cave was supposedly discovered by Perry in 1813. It is 208 feet long, 165 feet wide, and maintains a temperature of 42 degrees. The Wishing Well is a small lake within this cave.

Mammoth Cave, sixty feet underground, has an entrance that led to an eighty-by-sixty-foot lake. From there a six hundred foot tunnel led to a large cavern and the exit.

The six to thirty-two inches in length stalactites are the big attraction in Paradise Cave.

Crystal Cave is a deposit of celestite crystals composed of the compound Strontium Sulfate, the largest celestite crystals known in the world. In 1897 workmen were digging a well on

Gustav Heineman's property when they dug into a rock pocket lined with bluish white crystals. When they explored the opening, they found what is known to be the world's largest geods.

"Grape fever" seemed to run rampant on the Lake Erie islands. Put-in-Bay caught the fever around the middle of the 19th century. Some of the early growers were deRivera, Philip Vroman, Louis Harms, and Lorenz Miller. Others followed in their footsteps. Many of the growers came from Germany. Wineries sprang up along with the vineyards, the largest being the Put-in-Bay Wine Company organized in 1871. Unfortunately, in 1888 it went the route of many such wineries when a worker left an unattended fire in the office. Because of its destruction, many island business men were hurt financially.

Prohibition caused many wineries to cease operations; others sold unfermented grape juice. By the 1930s when the eighteenth amendment was repealed, very few wine makers remained on the island. Heineman's Winery, founded by Gustav Heineman, has continued in operation since 1901.

When Put-in-Bay Township was organized in 1861, South, Middle, and North Bass islands came under one school district. Philip Vroman had built the first schoolhouse on Put-in-Bay in 1855. It was in the central part of the island. Soon the population outgrew the building, and so Central School or "the school on the hill" was built. A special Put-in-Bay district was made in 1880, and it included Ballast, Rattlesnake, Gibraltar, Buckeye, and Starve Islands. Children, if any, from these small islands attended Put-in-Bay schools by boat or over the ice before the airplane came along.

Joel Oldt taught from August 1890 until 1908. While he was there, a high school was formed, graduating its first pupil, George J. Linskey, in 1895.

In 1904 the board of education decided to "bus" the children from East Point School to Central School during the months from November 14th until April 14th. This "bus" was either a wagon or sleigh, and it continued to run until 1918.

In the summer of 1921, a new building containing ten rooms, including an office, restrooms, a library, and a science laboratory was built on Catawba and Concord Avenues. This has served the island for many years and continues to do so.

During the 1850s, celebrations on Put-in-Bay attracted many visitors. At that time there weren't any overnight accommodations. Frederick Cooper built some guest rooms onto a grout house, took in a business partner, Andrew Decker, in 1867, and The Island Home was born. This venture underwent many changes, passed to several different owners, and acquired a new name almost every time the owner changed: from The Island Home to the Perry House, the Beebe House, and the Hotel Commodore which burned on August 23, 1932.

A.P. Edwards had built what was called the "White House." Joseph W. Gray, who was editor of the *Cleveland Plain Dealer*, purchased the "White House." After some additions were built and changes made, it became a hotel called "The Put-in-Bay House." This was big enough to accommodate eight hundred people in a rather luxurious fashion. There were dances, concerts, and other forms of entertainment provided for its guests. On the night that there was to be a grand ball held for the benefit of southern yellow fever victims, the hotel burned to the ground.

In 1889 Valentine Doller built a second smaller Put-in-Bay House on the site of the first one. It, too, burned in September of 1907.

In 1871 the Hunker House was built. This also changed names and ownership several times such as the Ward Summer Resort, the Detroit House, and the Crescent Hotel.

There were other hotels: the Park or Deutches Hotel, the Gill House, the Bay View House or Rendezvous, Conlen Cottage, Smith's Hotel, also known as Morgan's Hotel and Bayshore Hotel, Eagle Cottage or Friendly Inn now the Crew's Nest, and the Reibel House.

In December 1887, J.K. Tillotson of Toledo began the ground work for interested investors to build what became Hotel Victory at Stone's Cove. (This is now the location of South Bass Island State Park.) Building the Victory was a big undertaking. The hotel was to cover twenty-one acres. George Feick of Sandusky was the contractor. He not only had to build the hotel but a dining hall and dormitories for his seventy-five carpenters and other workmen as well as a sawmill and planing mill. Although guests arrived June 24th, 1892, the building wasn't completely finished until 1896. The Hotel Victory was an elaborate establishment such as the Lake Erie Islands had never seen and haven't seen since its demise. It claimed to be the largest summer hotel in America and attracted guests from many states. In Lydia J. Ryall's *Sketches and Stories of the Lake Erie Islands,* she describes the Victory in this way:

"The main building is in the form of a square and is 600 feet long by 300 feet deep; the main portion surrounding a court 3000 feet square.

"On one side, forming a wing and connected with the main building by a lobby, are the main dining hall, ordinary and kitchen, and back of these servants' quarters.

"The main dining hall is 155 feet long, 85 feet wide and 52 feet high, wide galleries encompassing the entire hall.

"The ordinary is 50 x 100 feet, and the combined dining capacity, including private banqueting halls and children's and nurses' dining hall, is 1,200 guests at one sitting. The guest chambers are 625 in number, large, light, airy and elegantly furnished, including 80 suites with baths. Every room fronts upon some lake view or toward the interior court, rendered charming with luxurious floral adornment, gravelled walks and other attractions.

"There are three elevators, bell boy stations on every floor, electric call bells, 6,000 incandescent electric lights, steam heating throughout the entire structure, and the most modern equipped hotel kitchen, it is said, in the world.

"A ramble through the big hotel is almost equal to that taken through a small town.

"Luxurious appointments are everywhere seen. The parlors of the Victory are numerous, showing varied styles of furniture and embellishment, each a model of elegance, comfort and luxury. Especially rich in upholstering are the ladies' grand parlors.

"The office, halls, lobbies and corridors are correspondingly magnificent, and in extent the place seems interminable, the combined length of the corridors alone being one mile, all handsomely carpeted.

"The main lobby—having a seating capacity of 1,000 persons—is a favored resort for hotel visitors when the hotel is open and running. Here the orchestra daily and nightly assembles, and music, mirth and festivity rule the hour. However, it is in the great ball room—by myriads of electric lights areaded, and brilliant as noonday—that representatives of social gaieties are more frequently found, joining in the grand promenade and mazy whirl.

"Others, again, seek the grand piazza, which extends the whole length of the main structure, where by day, or at night when illuminated with electricity, is found a breezy and most delightful place in which to doze and dream, or to hold social converse. From this outlook is afforded a scene upon which the eye may linger long without becoming weary, so charmingly picturesque, so restful and delightful, its environments.

"The grounds adjoining the hotel form a landscape garden which nature and art combine to beautify. Profuse but tasteful and exquisite floral decorations appear. Foliage plants and blooms of torrid richness blend with paler hues; while climbing the white walls and stone-pillared steps, masses of maderia, morning glory, nasturtium and woodbine spread a mantle of blossom-starred greenery. Care is taken to preserve natural effects, and in the park, consisting of twenty-one acres, extending to and along the shores of Victory bay, reveals a profusion of flowers, both wild and cultivated.

"A rustic bridge of artistic design spans the parks ravine; rough ledges of lime rock outcrop, and hollow stumps form receptacles for tender, blossoming plants and vines. An electric fountain sends aloft its jetting spray, and a cascaded board walk descends by gentle slope to the shore five hundred feet distant.

"The greatest charm of the park is its freedom, for the shore upon which it opens is as picturesques as ever conspired to woo the lover of Nature. Masses of beetling rock, of rock cleft and riven as by volcanic action, gird its broken line, while in the caverns, indenting their roughness, vines and mosses cover and shrubbery and cedar clumps edge and overdroop them.

"Boat and bathing houses occupy an eligible site, commanding a beach of smooth sand reached by a flight of steps. All the facilities for bathing are here afforded."

Even though Ms. Ryall has given us such a lavish description, from the beginning, the hotel was in financial trouble.

There were many unpaid bills, forcing the closing of the establishment several times. Finally, on August 14, 1919, because of a defective light wire, it went the way of many other island hotels and wineries, only this was probably the most expensive fire with an estimated loss of $450,000.

Once the tourist had arrived at Put-in-Bay, besides the usual wining and dining, fishing, bathing, and other activities connected with Lake Erie, he could find entertainment on a merry-go-round, watching military exercises and band concerts in the park, or visiting the Put-in-Bay museum, in which there was supposedly a collection of 10,000 items. Over the years many shops were established, carrying merchandise which attracted buyers, and today many people come to the Bay just to shop.

During the winter when much of Lake Erie has turned to ice, tourists who come are those interested in iceboating, skating, snowmobiling, and fishing through the ice. Fishing is best around the Bass Islands, Green Island, and Rattlesnake, as the ice is locked in that area. Most of the tourists fly in from Port Clinton, and for many years in the ice-fishing season the Ford Tri-Motor hauled thousands of passengers eager to try their luck. Islanders look forward to this time of year, as it means extra income for those who provide food, lodging, and services connected with the sport.

Probably the biggest tourist attraction of all at the Bay is what is commonly known as Perry's Monument. An act of Congress authorized the establishment of Perry's Victory and International Peace Memorial National Monument on Put-in-Bay on June 2, 1936. The Ohio State Legislature had authorized a study of the project in 1908. The Federal Government gave its assistance to the study in 1911. The memorial was constructed between October 1912 and June 1915 at the cost of approximately one million dollars. Nine states—Pennsylvania, Illinois, Wisconsin, Michigan, New York, Rhode Island, Kentucky, and Massachusetts—contributed to the project. The Perry's Victory Centennial Commission directed it.

The Milford granite of which the monument is constructed came from Massachusetts. There are seventy-eight courses of stone. It is in the form of a fluted Doric column 352 feet high and 45 feet in diameter at its base. The cap of it is an observation platform from which on a clear day one can see for many miles. A giant bronze urn 18 feet wide, 23 feet high, weighing eleven tons surmounts a penthouse above the observation platform. It is reported to be the greatest battle momument and the most massive column built by man.

Names of American ships and of the men wounded or killed in the battle are carved in the stone walls of the rotunda. Some historic tablets are also on the walls. The bodies of three American and three British officers killed in the battle were brought to lie beneath the floor of the rotunda from the shore of Put-in-Bay where they had been buried for one hundred years. This rotunda is made of Italian marble, granite, Indiana limestone, Tennessee marble, and bronze.

In addition to the War of 1812, Oliver Hazard Perry and the Battle of Lake Erie and consequently his monument, we can credit all of those early pioneers and those who came after to the South Bass Island that we know today.

# JOHN BROWN, JR.

In 1862 after his father, the abolitionist's execution, John Brown, Jr., his wife Wealthy, and their two children came to live on South Bass Island. There he became a vineyard keeper. His daughter Edith became the wife of T.B. Alexander, who was once Mayor of Put-in-Bay.

John Brown has been described as a kind and gentle man, very scholarly. He was interested in geology, phrenology, metaphysical science, and geometry which he taught to some of the island's young people.

John's brother Owen also came to Put-in-Bay. He was unmarried and somewhat of a recluse. He worked at Gibralter Island as a caretaker for Jay Cooke. When he learned of a needy family on the island, he often helped out in furnishing food and supplies. He, too, had been a prisoner, but he escaped from Harper's Ferry after the capture of his father.

Owen left Put-in-Bay with another brother Jason. They went to Pasadena, California to a Sierra Madre Mountain summit known as "Brown's Peak." Their sister Ruth Thompson lived in the valley. Owen died while he was visiting her and was buried on the mountain. Jason returned to Ohio. Although he went to Akron to live, he returned to Put-in-Bay to visit before his death.

John Brown, Jr. had been arrested in Kansas in 1854. He was forced to run nine miles with his arms tied behind him and his wrists bound. Because he lay in jail so tied for twenty-seven hours, he carried "slave bracelet" scars for the rest of his life.

John received the news that the *Island Queen* had been taken at Middle Bass by the Rebels. As soon as possible he recruited volunteers and set out for Catawba Island. The men were armed, probably with shotguns. When they reached Catawba they had to walk seven or eight miles and cross two channels of water in order to get to Johnson's Island. Arriving safely, Mr. Brown told Colonel Hill about the capture of the *Parsons* and the *Queen* and volunteered his men for duty.

John Brown, Jr. lived the remainder of his life on Put-in-Bay. He died in May of 1895. His wife lived until 1911. They are buried along with John Brown III, their daughter and her husband in the Put-in-Bay cemetery.

# NORTH BASS AND MIDDLE BASS ISLANDS

North Bass, four miles from Put-in-Bay, sixteen miles from Port Clinton, and twenty-four miles from Sandusky, was once called the Isle of St. George.

In the 1820s this island was part of Huron County and was known as Bass Island Number 3. An agent for the Connecticut Land Company, owner of the land, paid the yearly taxes. Title to the property was transferred to someone named Demming. Later it was transferred from Abigail Demming to Horace Kelley of Kelleys Island. There wasn't any permanent occupancy of the island until 1844 when Rosswell Nichols, his wife, and two brothers-in-law named Scott arrived. At first they were squatters. Then Nichols leased the land by paying the annual taxes. He was given one hundred fifty dollars by a Dr. Townsend who acted as agent for the owner who was then Champion. With this money he was to build a barn. Any other improvements he made were to be done at his own expense.

In 1849 Nichols purchased one hundred fourteen acres of the island at five dollars per acre. George Wires purchased one hundred thirty-seven acres. In 1853 Simon and Peter Fox came from Canada and purchased the remaining land.

Simon Fox planted grapes which grew well. Within a few years vineyards flourished. The fishing industry was a lucrative business which along with the grapes brought settlers.

There was a post office on North Bass before Middle Bass had one. Although the latter had applied for one, U.S. Government thought Middle Bass citizens could easily pick up their mail at Put-in-Bay. A young lady submitted to the government a picture she had painted to show the location of the various islands. Upon seeing its mistake, the government then granted Middle Bass a post office.

There is an elementary school on the island with one teacher. Children in the upper grades are flown on a daily basis to Put-in-Bay or the mainland for their education.

As there is an average of two hundred, frost-free growing days, twenty more than on the mainland, grapes are still thriving on North Bass. Meir's vineyards, owned by Meir's Wine Cellars of Silverton, Ohio, are located there. Around ten families live there and work in the vineyards.

Folkore claims that in the year 1680 Father Hennepin and his Jesuit Missionaries stopped at an island in Lake Erie and said Mass. This presumably was the first Christian service ever held on a Lake Erie island. It was spring with many wild flowers blooming there. These French explorers called the place Isle de Fleurs or in English Floral Island. Later it acquired the name of Middle Bass.

Today Middle Bass is well known for its winery. What we now call Lonz's was once the Golden Eagle Wine Company. A German immigrant named Wehrle established it in 1864. In one year the winery produced nearly 300,000 gallons of wine. Two of the largest casks in the United States were in use here, each one holding 16,000 gallons. On the 1200 acres of land, Wehrle built a magnificent house which later burned.

In 1867 another winery came into being on Middle Bass. Joseph Miller, who had raised grapes in Germany, left his home in Baden in 1854 to come to the United States. For three years he lived near Cedar Point and then came to Middle Bass where he started the Bretz Winery.

Enough people came to this island to settle for year around living that the citizens built a school, an island hall, established a post office, and the Middle Bass Club for fishing and boating enthusiasts. Presidents Cleveland and Harrison as well as senators and governors were guests of the club. Governor Bushnell once owned a cottage on Middle Bass Island.

# GIBRALTER ISLAND

Gibralter Island lies between East Point and Peach Point off South Bass Island. Two graves bearing the inscription "James Ross—Died August 11, 1848" and "John Elliott—Died September 18th, 1848," were there when Joseph DeRivera St. Jurgo purchased the Bass Islands in 1854. Gibralter Island came with the lot of them. No one knows the background of these men.

This island supposedly shields Put-in-Bay Harbor from west and northwest winds, making it a safe refuge for boats. Also, supposedly, Commodore Perry used Gibralter as a lookout before the battle of 1812.

The Civil War financier Jay Cooke purchased the island from DeRivera St. Jurgo in 1864 for $3,000 and used it for family and friends' vacations. Cooke was born in Sandusky, Ohio in 1821, but he moved to Philadelphia, Pennsylvania, where he met Salmon P. Chase who served as Secretary of the Treasury under Abraham Lincoln. It was through this connection that he became involved with Civil War finances.

After making his fortune, he became interested in the Lake Erie islands where he had fished and hunted in his youth. After he had acquired Gibralter, he built an elaborate castle-type Victorian home there. The windows and doors for this home were aboard the *Island Queen* when it was overtaken by Rebel pirates during the Civil War. Although the *Queen* was partially sunk on Chick-a-nole reef, it was raised and the windows and doors were saved. As Cooke was deeply religious, he entertained not only the rich and famous but also the less fortunate pastors from small congregations, paying for their entire vacations including transportation.

Jay Cooke passed away in 1905, having been able to enjoy life on his beloved island for almost forty years. His family kept the property until 1925 when it sold to a Columbus industrialist, Julius F. Stone.

Stone deeded the island to Ohio State University as the Franz Theodore Stone Laboratory, or Stone Lab as it's called, in honor of his father. The University moved its main research operations there, built a concrete lab, a dining hall, and a cottage for university trustees. Operated by OSU's College of Biological Sciences, it is one of the oldest fresh water field biology stations in the United States. There are classes held in botany, entomology, and zoology.

During the 1950s, most of Stone Lab's faculty went back to Columbus, and the university used the island's facilities for summer sessions only. Winter transportation costs by airplane had become too expensive. There was even talk of closing the Lab altogether. The so-called "death of Lake Erie" came to its rescue.

In 1970, OSU set up the Center for Lake Erie Area Research. This was to co-ordinate programs of many of Ohio's colleges and universities doing research on the lake. A federal grant was received to study the lake and to educate its users. Because of this activity, Gibralter came alive again. Jay Cooke's Victorian castle became a dormitory for budding biologists, many from out-of-state and some from foreign countries. There are women students, too.

Gibralter is not open to tourists.

# THE FORD TRI-MOTOR

Although the Ford Tri-Motor appeared on the commercial airline scene in the 1920s, it wasn't until the 1930s that it became a mainstay of the Lake Erie Islanders' way of life and remained so for many years. This is a large metal plane about 51 feet long with a 75-foot wing span. It can take off unloaded in less than one hundred yards. It has three 235 horse power engines, one on the nose and one on the side underneath each wing. The plane can maintain level flight with only one engine and can fly on two as well as three engines. It has a cruising speed of from eighty-five to one hundred miles an hour. Though called a Tin goose, many see it as something different with one man saying, "It looks more like a tin shed than a goose to me." Depending upon the model, it can carry from twelve to seventeen passengers, more sometimes, as I've been on one when there were as many as twenty passengers.

One can't write or talk about the islands' Tin Goose without mentioning the man responsible for bringing it to Lake Erie, Milton Hershberger. Hershberger, as he was usually referred to by islanders, was born in Anderson, Indiana. There he learned to fly, working as a pilot's helper in exchange for flying lessons. He became a test pilot and managed airports in Chicago, Youngstown, and Sandusky, Ohio. In February 1929, carrying one passenger, Reverend Joseph E. Maerder, a priest who served both Kelleys Island and Put-in-Bay Catholic churches, Hershberger landed a plane at Put-in-Bay. He had flown from Sandusky in a plane owned by Parker Brothers. This was such an awesome occasion that school was dismissed so that the children could watch.

After this flight, he organized his own company, Erie Isle Airways. He spent his life's savings to purchase fifty acres of land which became Put-in-Bay's airport. The superstructure of the hangar was brought across the ice from Kelleys Island one winter. He later acquired the Port Clinton Airport into which he made daily trips. On November 11, 1930, flying a three-place Waco biplane, he made his first flight from his airport to the mainland with Roy Webster as his first passenger.

When he first began his commercial venture, he didn't have the mail contract, but he helped Kelleys Island's mail carrier during impossible ice conditions and flew the mail to the mainland. Later he was given a contract for year-round service by air to all of the U.S. Lake Erie Islands.

In May 1934, he was flying alone in a Standard biplane when the engine flew apart. He, along with seven bags of mail, landed in the water near Lakeside. A commercial fish boat came to his rescue.

Will Haas was Put-in-Bay's telegraph operator for fifty years. He offered Hershberger the money needed to purchase his first Tri-Motor. In time he was to own seven of them. By 1935, he had acquired five. At this time, he changed the name of his airline to Island Airways.

For many years Hershberger and his Tin Goose were the lifeline of the islands. They carried passengers, mail, supplies, clergymen, doctors, the ill, and yes, the dead. Many funeral processions flew in the Tin Goose. It was also a school bus, flying children from Middle and North Bass and Rattlesnake Island to Put-in-Bay on a daily basis.

In August 1953, the barnstorming pilot who had become an island legend, sold his airline to Ralph Dietrick from Sandusky. It's been said that from the time he sold the airline, he never again set foot on his Port Clinton airfield and he never again piloted a plane, although he lived to be eighty-five years old.

The corporate title of the business became Sky Tours, Inc., and the name Island Airways was changed to Island Airlines. Ralph expanded the business and operated out of both Sandusky and Port Clinton to all of the islands until 1962, when he sold his Sandusky interest to Sue and Harry Griffing. He then concentrated on flying from Port Clinton to the Bass Islands. His airline sometimes ran fourteen scheduled trips a day. In one year it carried 35,000 passengers, 300,000 pounds of cargo, and 135,000 pounds of mail. One unusual piece of freight was a 20-foot long timber needed on Middle Bass for a boat yard. One end of the timber was stuck in the cockpit, and the other end stuck out the open door in the side of the plane.

After Hershberger had sold his airline, troubles began to plague the Tri-Motor. July 31, 1954, one of the big birds crashed at Kelleys Island with the pilot sustaining serious injuries. August 21, 1972, another one crashed when an engine failed on take-off at Port Clinton. There were only minor injuries. July 1, 1977, was doomsday for the flight of the Tin Goose as far as service to the islands was concerned. Pilot Dave Martin crashed taking off from the Put-in-Bay airport about 1:45 in the afternoon. He was hospitalized with serious injuries, though his two passengers, Russell and Romana Childers from Port Orchard, Washington, were treated and released from a hospital. The cause of the crash was attributed to fuel line problems and a sudden gust of wind.

In 1973 Ralph Dietrick sold Island Airlines to some men from Mansfield, Ohio. Dave Haberman then became owner-manager, president of the company. Dave sent the remains of the Tin Goose to Kalamazoo, Michigan Municipal Airport for repairs. It was there for nearly three years with Kal Aero Company doing the work on it. The skin on the fuselage was replaced with new alloy metals, the cockpit was rebuilt, electric fuel pumps replaced the gravity feed that was once used. The cost to rebuild was approximately $300,000.

Federal regulations will no longer allow the Tri-Motor to land at the islands. The company used the plane for sight-seeing trips over the islands when it returned to its home base at Port Clinton. In November of 1980, Island Airline pilots Harold Hauck and Ed Rusch flew the Goose to Orlando, Florida to give daily sight-seeing trips over Disney World.

In 1985 the "shortest airline in the world" relinquished its claim to the Tin Goose. Al Chaney of Hebron, Ohio purchased it and took it off on a tour of forty-eight states, telling its story and of its association with the Lake Erie Islands to all who would listen.

My husband and I have some very personal memories of the old plane. During the 1950s when Ralph Dietrick owned Island airlines, Ralph along with my husband, Howard Brown from Kelleys Island, Sue Hively from Sandusky, and a Mr. Gill from Port Clinton, flew one of the Tri-Motors which Ralph had purchased from Phoenix, Arizona to the Port Clinton airport. My husband felt that as a pilot he could ask for no bigger thrill than to manipulate the big metal bird between mountains of the Southwest and over the flatlands on their way to Ohio. What a welcoming home party there was when they landed on that Port Clinton runway!

In the 1940s, the Tin Goose flew two daily schedules into Kelleys Island, one at mail time (around 9:30 A.M.), the other in late afternoon. The first airplane ride I ever had was on a Tin Goose from Kelleys Island to Port Clinton. Around this time I was having treatments by physicians in Cleveland, Ohio for a skin ailment. For reasons too detailed to tell, these treatments needed to be scheduled at 9:00 o'clock on Saturday morning. To make this appointment, I had to leave Kelleys Island on a Friday afternoon plane schedule to Port Clinton, travel to Cleveland by train, stay there overnight, have my treatment, return to Port Clinton by train, and via plane to Kelleys Island on Saturday afternoon. The pilot soon recognized me as a regular Friday customer.

One Friday afternoon he called me from the island's airport to say that he had come early as fog was setting in, and he thought by late afternoon all planes could be grounded. I was at the airport ten minutes after he called. When we took off, no one else was on that plane but the pilot and me. We were airborne for only two minutes when fog completely engulfed us. There was no radar to guide us in to either Port Clinton or Put-in-Bay or back to Kelleys Island. There was radio contact, but it was difficult to tell exactly where over Lake Erie we were flying. We circled for some twenty minutes. In that time my thoughts were varied. Frankly, I was scared half to death. I knew that our fuel supply wouldn't go on forever. Just when I was ready to scribble some last minute instructions for posterity, my pilot caught a glimpse of Perry's Monument. That great historical marking helped to serve as a bearing to get us into Put-in-Bay's airport. Those at the airport were greatly amazed that anyone could find his way in such a thick fog.

I stayed over night at Milton Hershberger's home on Put-in-Bay. By the next morning, the temperature had dropped considerably and the sun was unusually bright with not a trace of fog. As it was too late for me to keep my appointment in Cleveland, I returned to Kelleys Island on the mail schedule. I had traveled only ten or twelve miles each way. Needless to say I've been forever grateful that Admiral Oliver Hazard Perry fought and won the Battle of Lake Erie.

# LIFE FLIGHT

Norbert McKillips was police chief of Kelleys Island for twenty some years. On December 9th, 1983, he suffered a heart attack. Those attending him called a Life Flight plane from Toledo, Ohio to transport him to a hospital on the mainland, but because of weather conditions the plane had to return to the airport.

For generations, when an islander became ill enough to need hospital care, there were many ways to get him to the mainland—by boat, in a sled over the ice, in an open car over the ice, and in recent years by calling one of the pilots of the airlines which served the island. However, because of modern terms such as malpractice suits and liabilities, physicians are reluctant to send off a patient unless someone associated with medical personnel is with him.

When the Toledo plane turned back, and Mr. McKillip's condition had not improved, an Island Airways plane, a six-seat Cessna, piloted by Bob Rigoni, who was also a sargeant with Port Clinton Police Department, took off from Put-in-Bay around 9:00 P.M. Along with Mr. Rigoni were an Ottawa County Sheriff's deputy and paramedic thirty-six years old Bruce Mettler, Put-in-Bay emergency medical service personnel Dwayne Dress who was fifty years old, and Mike Sweeney, twenty years old. Their mission was to try to stabilize the condition of Chief McKillips.

Around 10:00 P.M. the Coast Guard received notice that the plane was missing. Two Coast Guard boats from Marblehead were dispatched to search the lake. Pilot Rigoni had radioed from the plane that there was zero visibility. There was a fog bank lying north of a line from Perry's Monument to Kelleys Island's stone dock. South of that visibility was three or four miles.

On Saturday, December 10th, along with the Coast Guard boats, private boats, a helicopter sent from Detroit, a state partol plane, Island Airway's planes, a salvage boat from Schrock's Marina, and personnel from Erie County Recovery Team, all took part in searching Lake Erie around the islands' area. People from Kelleys Island furnished sandwiches, soup, and hot coffee to those out on the lake.

On Saturday afternoon the plane was found three miles south of Ballast Island in thirty-two feet of water. Although the men weren't in the plane, Rigoni's jacket and a paramedic's box were. The wreckage appeared to be a "gentle" crash. The men probably had time to unbuckle their seat belts and get out. According to one of the searchers, one of the plane's doors was open, and a window looked as if it had been kicked out. A salvage boat piloted by Neil Schrock from Schrock's Marina brought the plane up and into the marina to wait for Federal Aviation Administration examiners.

The search for the men continued on Sunday, but only the pilot's log book was found. Gale force winds and waves averaging seven feet called a halt to the lake's activity. On Monday, December 12th, sometime between 2:00 P.M. and 4:30 P.M. all four bodies were found about seventy-five feet from the crash site. The bodies showed no visible signs of injury.

Funeral services for Mettler, Dress, and Sweeney were held at Put-in-Bay on Friday, December 16th. One hundred uniformed officials saluted as pall bearers carried the caskets into the Mother-of-Sorrows Church. U.S. Representative Delbert Latta from Bowling Green, Ohio read a letter from President Ronald Reagan which said, "Nancy and I send our prayers and heartfelt sympathy to all those gathered on this solemn occasion. The men you honor this morning are heroes—Americans who were dedicated to the safety of their fellow men and who in the last full measure of their devotion to duty gave their lives so that another might live. May the Good Lord bless and be with the families and friends who have come together to mourn their loss. God bless you." Governor Celeste flew to Put-in-Bay to console the families. Because of bad weather, some mainlanders couldn't attend the funeral. A special memorial service was held with more than three hundred people in attendance at Island Airways Airport in Port Clinton. On Friday, December 16th, at 10:00 A.M., services were held for Bob Rigoni at the Immaculate Conception Hall in Port Clinton.

When a plane didn't arrive at Kelleys Island on Friday, December 8th to take care of Police Chief McKillips, a helicopter from Cleveland Metropolitan General Hospital came and took him to a hospital in Sandusky. Not many days after the air tragedy had occurred, Chief McKillips, also, passed away as a result of his heart condition.

# THE SMALLER ISLANDS

In addition to the larger Bass islands, Johnson Island, Kelleys, and Pelee, there are many smaller islands whose inhabitants, were they alive, would have tales to tell. Upon hearing the names of some these islands, one might think he is in a farm yard. There are Mouse Island, Hen, Big Chicken and Little Chicken, and Chickenolee Reef. There are Starve Island, Gull Island, Middle Island, Sugar Island, Rattlesnake, East Sister, Middle Sister, North Harbor, Ballast, Lost Ballast, and Green Islands, some of them in the United States; some, in Canada.

Middle Island, located just north of the international border, is Canada's southernmost outpost. During prohibition days, rum runners used it as a stopping point. Middle Island also served as a lighthouse station where government employees who kept the lights burning lived. Once during the winter a lone occupant of the island, with only his dog for company, survived a serious illness, lying for several days with no care.

East Sister and Middle Sister, Hen and Chicken Islands, and North Harbor are all Canadian. North Harbor, one of the smallest, is located close to East Sister.

James Morrison of Put-in-Bay purchased East Sister several years ago. He built a house there for his wife and four sons, did some fishing and farming. As he owned a pound boat, he was able to take his home grown produce to the other islands to sell. Although only a few acres of soil make up the island, there must have been enough to provide for his family.

For many years Hen and the Chicken Islands were

uninhabited. The Hen, six acres of mostly rock, is located six miles west of Pelee with the Chickens about a mile south of the "mother." This is an excellent fishing area. The Canadian Government owned the islands until the 1880s when a Mr. L. McDonald of London, Ontario purchased Hen. He sold it to Captain Dennis Blanchard and Norman Andrews of Birmingham, Ohio in 1883 for the price of $250. Captain Blanchard was known as "the hermit of the old Hen," but he didn't live like a hermit. He helped to clear land on his island, planted grapes and peach trees, and built a house where he entertained many friends. There he lived for twelve summers.

In 1895 four men from Sandusky, James Saunderson, Henry Foster, August Feitel, and John Feick, bought a part of the island. They formed a fishing club called the Quinnebog Club of which there were sixteen charter members. In 1897 the club purchased the rest of the island. They built a dock and building with a kitchen and dining room. Membership in the club grew, and a stock company formed. Proceeds from this built a dormitory and a club house and installed water and gas lights. For several years the club served as a recreational facility for its members. However, when recreational boating became popular, the club's popularity decreased to nothing.

West Sister, which is west of Port Clinton, is a game preserve. In the early 1850s, one Dr. Girty, a brother of Simon Girty, lived on West Sister. Once there were two men, two women, and a child who were French Canadian living there. The child died during the winter. The men placed its body in a boat and started out across the ice for burial at their Canadian home land. At some point along the way the ice broke, and the two men drowned, leaving their women stranded on West Sister for several weeks with very few supplies. When navigation season opened, they were able to hail a passing boat and return home.

Early in the twentieth century, supposedly a sailor was stranded on a two acre mass of rocks and little growth in the United States' waters of Lake Erie. When his skeleton was found, it was assumed he had starved to death, thus the name Starve Island for that little piece of land.

Green Island was once call Strontian Island. It is located

about one mile west of Put-in-Bay. It is made up of twenty acres of land which is government property and on which is located a lighthouse. The first lighthouse on Green Island burned on New Year's Day 1862. Col. Drake was the keeper at the time and lived there with his wife and children. It had been a warm day that suddenly turned to twenty-five degrees below zero. A group of young people including Col. Drake's son Pitt were at a party on Put-in-Bay when they saw the fire. Because of the severe storm, no one was able to reach Green Island until the next day. People were amazed that the Drakes hadn't died from cold weather or the fire but were keeping warm together under a feather bed in a building where a cow was stabled.

Rattlesnake Island's name is misleading as there are no rattlesnakes on the island. There may have been at one time, although to my knowledge that hasn't been confirmed. Some claim it was so named becaused of its shape. It is about two miles from South Bass and is made up of about twenty acres. It has the distinction of having the nation's only private airmail service and even has its own postage stamp. Any children living on the island are transported by plane or boat to other schools, usually to Put-in-Bay. As the island changes ownership from time-to-time, one wonders what future development might come to this little spot of land.

Tiny three acre Mouse Island is very close to Catawba Point. It, too, is privately owned and once belonged to a President of the United States, Rutherford B. Hayes. He and his family spent many summers there.

It has been said that Ballast Island received its name from the idea that Admiral Perry took ballast stones from the quarry there for his fleet. Some historians say that isn't true. Perry's log book might contain the truth. A small part of Ballast was cut off from the main island several years ago by wind and waves. This is called "Lost Ballast."

For thirty-five years, one Lem Brown owned Ballast Island. At that time there was an old fisherman whom everyone knew as "Uncle Jimmy" who lived alone there. He usually went to Put-in-Bay in his small boat for supplies. One day, however, he boarded a steamer for Sandusky. The steamer blew up, and Uncle Jimmy died as a result of burns.

The island later became the property of a stock company consisting of some prominent people. George W. Gardner, one time partner of John D. Rockefeller and one time Mayor of Cleveland, was one of them. A canoe club was organized, and races were held. A club house and some cottages and even a church were built.

Gull Island is a little more than a mile north of Kelleys Island. It's more often called a reef or a shoal. Sea gulls nest on this spot each spring, thus the name.

During the early 1960s, six duck hunters, one a professional guide on Lake Erie, were hunting on Middle and Gull Island, which is only about fifty feet long and fifteen feet wide. It extends above the water about three feet. There they had built a blind. They had secured their provisions on Middle Island not far away and anchored their larger boat between it and Gull. The guide and another man had gone to the reef in an aluminum skiff. Although the weather had begun to turn a little threatening, it seemed perfect for duck hunting.

Pulling the skiff onto the reef, they piled rocks and debris around it for their blind, they soon became too pre-occupied with knocking down their prey that they didn't pay attention to the weather. Suddenly the wind and rain struck with a fury. There was a lull, and then it came again more brutal than at first. Waves broke over the reef, threatening to wash the men away. When there was a second lull, after three unsuccessful attempts, they finally started the motor on the skiff and set out for their larger boat. It had broken loose, and they were at first unable to see it. Unfortunately, when they did locate it, their skiff ran out of fuel. After about two hours of rowing, they reached the larger boat. The temperature had dropped to 16 degrees F. Changing from the skiff to the other boat for awhile seemed impossible in such a sea, but eventually this was accomplished.

Trying to find a place on Middle Island to dock the boat during such a storm was difficult. The guide left it in the hands of the other man and got into the skiff. A huge wave picked up this aluminum object and deposited it and its captain on top of a cliff. Those men left on Middle Island, assuming they would never see the others alive again, were amazed to see their guide.

One of the hunters had developed a fever. They decided to

go to Pelee Island, about five miles away, for help. Again they had to row the skiff to the larger boat, taking one man at a time. One of the men had broken both legs previously and had to be carried across land to the skiff.

Getting from Middle Island to Pelee was a treacherous task. Waves nearly overturned the boat, and ice was forming everywhere. Fearing they would sink with the icy weight, they kept chipping away. They reached South Bay on Pelee around 8:00 o'clock P.M.

The next day some of the hunters flew back to Ohio; the others had to wait five days until the ice in the harbor broke up. Even then, before they reached home port, the Coast Guard had to free them from an ice jam about two hundred yards from shore. So you see, even tiny Gull Island has a tale to tell.

# JOHNSON'S ISLAND

This island lies about three miles across from Sandusky, Ohio and one-half mile from Marblehead Peninsula's Bay Point. Except for the Confederate Cemetery on the east point, it is made up of three hundred acres of land about one mile long and one-half mile wide. It was called Bull's Island until 1852 when L.B. Johnson of Sandusky purchased the island.

During the Civil War the United States Government was looking for a prison site to house Confederate prisoners. Colonel William Hoffman was assigned the job of finding such a place. He learned that half of Johnson's Island could be leased for $500 per year with control over the whole area. Its isolation recommended it as a safe spot. The government approved. Speculations for necessary buildings were soon on the drawing board, and on November 15th, 1861, William T. West and Philander Gregg signed contracts to do the work for a sum of $30,000. By February of 1862 there was a prison erected on Johnson's Island with completion of it done before the end of that year. Forty acres had been converted into barracks, a hospital, and buildings for a quartermaster and commissary stores.

During the war ten thousand prisoners were in the barracks, with three thousand the maximum at one time. Practically all the prisoners were officers, prominent professional men, and rich plantation owners. Some of them recorded in their diaries that they were exposed to many hardships: poor rations of food, pneumonia, diphtheria, small pox, and southern clothing unsuitable for harsh northern winters. Two hundred six men died and were buried on Johnson's Island while imprisoned there.

There were many plots from time to time to free these prisoners. One almost succeeded. Confederate Commander Jacob Thompson had assigned a Major C.H. Cole to lead such a mission. He came to Sandusky, posing as a Pennsylvania oil operator and rented living quarters at a rooming house called West House. Also at the rooming house were a young, attractive woman named Annie and a man named John Y. Beall, who had a part in the conspiracy. There has been little truthful information learned about Cole and Annie's background or about their life after the Civil War. They seemed to have faded into oblivion.

However, John Beall was from Walnut Grove, Virginia, a graduate of the University of Virginia. He joined the Confederate Army as a private in the Second Virginia Infantry and was wounded at Harper's Ferry. While he was recuperating from this wound, he devised a plan to act as a privateer on the Great Lakes or Eastern seaboard. Confederate President Jefferson Davis commissioned him as Acting Master of the Confederate Navy, approving him as a privateer on eastern waters.

A Scotsman named Bennett G. Burleigh (Burley) had brought plans for his invention of submarines and mines from Scotland to the United States. He had been a warrior and a seaman. He met Beall and went to work with him in the Chesapeake Bay area. Both men were captured in November of 1863 and held prisoners, but they were exchanged in May of 1864. When released, they went to Canada to see a Colonel Thompson in Toronto. He advised them of plans to free Johnson Island's prisoners. Beall then went to Sandusky to talk with Cole and then went back to Windsor to get some men to help him.

Clement Vallandigham of Ohio, who was a former Congressman and an unsuccessful candidate for Governor of Ohio, was head of the Sons of Liberty (known as Copperheads). Col. Thompson thought he had Vallandigham's help, and he informed Cole that an army of Copperheads would show up in Sandusky to help in the plot. This didn't happen.

Three boats were involved in their scheme. The Union's

man-of-war *Michigan* was based in Sandusky Bay under the command of Captain Jack Carter. Cole met Carter and lavished him and his crew with wine and good food. Carter in return gave him a complete tour of the *Michigan*, the first iron war ship in the world, little suspecting a plan to seize the boat, free the prisoners, and use it to sack every city on the western Great Lakes.

Beall's part in the plot was to board the *Philo Parsons,* a lake passenger ship from Detroit that stopped at the islands and Sandusky. His teammate Burleigh was part of the plan. Burleigh went to the docks in Detroit on September 18, 1864, to talk with Walter O. Ashley, part owner and clerk of the *Parsons*. He told Ashley that he had planned a pleasure trip with some friends who wanted to go to Kelleys Island. However, they were at Sandwich on the Canadian side, and one friend was lame. He wanted the *Parsons* to pick them up there. Ashley agreed to do this, but he informed Burley that they couldn't bring any baggage as there wasn't a custom office at Kelleys Island.

On September 19th, the *Parsons* left at 8:00 A.M. and picked up the passengers at Sandwich. It also picked up some men at Malden in Canada who were going to Sandusky. One man limped and wore a Kossuth hat. They brought with them a heavy box bound with rope.

The *Parsons* stopped at Put-in-Bay and Middle Bass Island where the ferry's captain Sylvester Atwood lived. The captain went ashore, turning the *Parsons* over to D.C. Nichols, his first mate. The next stop was Kelleys Island. Clerk Ashley reminded Burleigh that this was where he and his friends wanted to go, but Burleigh said they had decided to go on to Sandusky.

The *Island Queen* was a ferry that carried prisoners to Johnson's Island as well as passengers to the other islands. She and the *Parsons* passed within a hundred yards of each other. Shortly afterwards, the man who limped and wore the Kossuth hat stepped up to the first mate Nichols and ordered him at gunpoint to pilot the boat to a spot near the Marblehead lighthouse. This man was Beall. Four armed men confronted Clerk Ashley and told him that he'd be shot if he made a move. The box they had brought on board contained enough guns to arm twenty-five or thirty men. Passengers were told that the ship was in command of the Confederates and were put in the hold as captives. The engineer, James Denison, fireman Michael Campbell, and Nichols were ordered to their posts.

It was discovered that the *Parsons'* fuel supply was low, and Nichols was ordered to take it back to Middle Bass for wood. There the Rebels told the men to load the wood onto the boat. When they refused to do this, there was some gun play. A young boy ran for Captain Atwood telling him to come quick as someone was shooting at his father who operated the wood yard. The Confederates then grabbed Atwood and shoved him helpless aboard his boat.

The *Island Queen* had picked up passengers at Kelleys Island and was preparing to dock at Middle Bass, but the *Parsons* was in her place. She tied alongside. Some of her crewmen jumped aboard the *Parsons* to facilitate tying the *Queen* and were taken prisoners. The Rebels then took control of the *Queen* and its Captain Orr as well. The engineer Henry Haines was shot in the nose, cheek and ear, bound and thrown onto the *Parsons*. When they realized they couldn't operate the boat without him, the Rebels brought him back aboard. There were twenty-five Union soldiers on vacation aboard the *Queen*. They, too, were taken prisoners and ordered to load the wood. They did so. Then after promising to never take up arms against the Confederacy again, they were set free on Middle Bass along with the other passengers and Captain Atwood. Then the *Parsons* cast off with the *Queen* in tow.

One of Beall's men knocked off the *Queen's* "pony valve" with a sledge hammer so that water could flow into the hold. She was then set adrift between Middle Bass and Kelleys Island to sink. The *Parsons* proceeded to the Marblehead lighthouse to await a signal for Cole as planned. The signal didn't come.

It so happened that two days before the *Philo Parsons* left Detroit an informer had walked into the Provost Office there with details of a plan to take the *Michigan*. The office personnel sent a telegram to Captain Jack Carter warning him of danger. Carter replied that he doubted such danger existed but that he would be ready if it did. Then he sent an Ensign Eddy to West House in Sandusky to see if he could learn of any strange activities. There he found suspicious papers that the girl Annie had carelessly left in Cole's room. Another telegram came to Carter telling him that men would leave Malden, seize either the *Parsons* or another steamer bound for Kelleys Island, that officers and men had been bought by a man named Cole, some men were to be introduced on board under the disguise of friends, and an officer named Eddy was to be drugged. After reading the telegram, Carter immediately contacted Colonel Charles Hill in charge of Johnson's Island.

Captain Carter decided he had no choice but to arrest Cole. He knew he'd have to be careful as he wasn't sure if the information received was accurate or if this was the right Cole. He sent an ensign and a provost marshall to bring Cole from Sandusky to the *Michigan* telling Cole the Captain wanted to see him. Colonel Hill joined Carter.

Cole went on deck of the ship and started to light a cigar, which act was supposed to have been the signal for Beall and his crew to take the iron war ship. A Union soldier from Johnson's Island stepped forward and arrested him.

Colonel Hill questioned Cole about the papers which Ensign Eddy had found in his room at West House. Cole admitted he had acted as a Confederate agent in Sandusky along with Abraham Strain, Dr. Ellwood Stanley, John M. Brown, John H. Williams, Louis Rosenthal, E. Merrick, and John Robinson. Hill returned to the island to send a detachment of his troops to Sandusky to seal off the harbor. Orders were issued to guards to detain all passengers arriving by train. The soldiers questioned the men Cole had named, arrested them, and brought them to the *Michigan* where Cole remained a prisoner for awhile. Later he was transferred to Johnson's Island.

Meanwhile, the Rebels aboard the *Parsons* were becoming uneasy. Beall wanted the men to go into Sandusky Bay, but they refused. He wanted them to attack the *Michigan*. He took a vote on such action: two voted yea; seventeen voted against it. Beall considered his men a bunch of cowards. He presented a document for them to each sign stating that he was a gentleman and a soldier and admitting their refusal to obey him. Around midnight he ordered the boat to turn around and head for Detroit.

As the boat came close to Middle Bass, it ran into a fish net, and Nichols had to get it free. As it came near Malden about dawn, he was ordered to steer toward the Canadian channel, starboard of Fighting Island. Most of the crew and passengers that were still aboard were left on this island. When the *Parsons* docked at Sandwich, Ontario, the Rebels began to unload everything aboard that they could carry. They began walking North toward Windsor, leaving the *Parsons* to sink at the dock.

At sunrise on the morning after Cole was arrested, Captain Carter took the *Michigan* to look for the *Parsons*. He stopped at Kelleys Island where he was told about the activities concerning the *Parsons* and the *Island Queen*, though no one knew for sure what had happened. He then steered toward Put-in-Bay. On the way there he met Clerk Ashley and some of the *Parson's* crew in a sailboat who told their story. He continued on to Detroit, but no one there knew where the boats were, and so he went back to Put-in-Bay. Finally, at 1:20 P.M. the *Queen* was sighted half submerged on Chick-a-nole Reef between Kelleys Island and Pelee. Carter returned to the Sandusky Bay.

The *Parsons* and the *Queen* were both raised from the water within a few days. As there was little damage, they both resumed their ferry service.

Beall was captured near Niagara Falls and was charged with spying and piracy. He was hanged on February 24, 1865.

Burleigh was arrested in Canada. He was extradited to the United States but wasn't tried for war crimes. Instead he was charged with stealing forty dollars from the *Parson's* clerk at Middle Bass. His trial was held at Port Clinton. The jury couldn't agree on whether or not he was guilty. He was jailed at Port Clinton, but he escaped and went back to Scotland. After the war Cole was sent from Johnson's Island to Fort Lafayette in New York from which he was released on February 10, 1866.

When the war ended, Johnson's Island was abandoned. The Prison's buildings were auctioned off and used as cottages for summer people. In the 1890s a summer resort flourished there, but Cedar Point soon became a more popular place. There was some farming done as well as quarrying.

In the early part of the century some Sicilian stone quarry workers lived in the abandoned shacks near the cemetery where the prisoners had been buried. During a severe storm in the spring, the men became afraid and ran out of these buildings and huddled close to a bronze statue which the Ohio Daughters had erected in 1910. Suddenly they heard a bugle call. The statue turned toward the graves (so they reported) from which arose a company of gray clad soldiers. Each one silently shouldered a musket, marched off, and disappeared. The next day the Sicilians rowed ashore, told their tale, and refused to return to the island.

Years later a causeway bridge extending from the Marblehead Peninsula and residences on waterfront lots were built. Today the island is a private place except for the cemetery which is open to visitors. For many years the cemetery was abandoned. Then in 1889 officials from Georgia raised funds to place Georgia marble headstones on each of the 206 graves. For over forty years Anton Johannsen of Sandusky was caretaker.

# PELEE'S McCORMICK FAMILY

David McCormick, a Scotchman, and his wife bore six children. Their youngest son Alexander was an adventurous soul. In 1761 he and an older brother came to the New World. The older brother went to the Carolinas, but Alexander stayed in Philadelphia where he worked for a merchant. Around 1768 he decided to move on and joined a band of traders.

Although we don't know whether or not he was captured, we know that for ten years he lived with Shawnee Indians. He must have earned the respect of the red man, because the chief gave him his sister for a wife. The two had a son whom they named David. Although the wife died a few years later, Alexander took good care of his son.

The Shawnee tribe moved into the Maumee Valley where Toledo, Ohio now is, taking Alexander as their business manager. He often traveled back and forth between there and Detroit to trade furs.

One day a tribe of Wyandotte's came into the valley with a beautiful young white girl whom they had captured at Fort Pitt. Her name was Elizabeth Turner. There had been two families, the McKevar's and the Turner's, who were neighbors in Fort Pitt. They had joined together in making a sugar camp for processing maple sap into sugar. Their two young sons worked at the camp to keep the sap boiling properly.

One day Elizabeth Turner, a McKevar girl, and her small brother took some provisions to the boys at the camp. The girls heard two rifle shots and saw the two boys fall dead. Some savages seized the girls and the small brother and dragged them

115

into the woods. The girls were separated, and the McKevar girl was never found. The Indians killed the little boy. However, they admired Elizabeth's spunk and courage and treated her well. They called her *Chest-nut Burr* because her actions sometimes stung like a burr. The only time they accused her of being a coward was the time she made an excuse to search for a horse in the woods. She didn't want to watch them torture and execute Colonel Crawford, whom they believed was Elizabeth's father.

The Wyandottes brought Elizabeth with them into the Maumee Valley. Here she and Alexander McCormick met and soon fell in love. He tried to persuade her captors to release her to him and even offered them a valuable ransom. However, when he went to claim her, they refused to let her go.

Alexander planned to take furs to Detroit. Elizabeth decided to join him. She lay flat in the canoe, and he piled heavy furs on top of her. The Indians came searching. Even though they removed some of the furs and tramped on the others, they decided she wasn't with him, and they left. The two lovers went to the home of Alexander's friend, Colonel Allen, in Detroit. There they were married in May, 1783.

They went back to the Maumee Valley where Alexander's son David was and established a trading post.

In May, 1784, a son William was born. Later seven other children were born to this union. In 1795, Alexander moved his family to Malden Township, Essex County, in Canada. He passed away in 1803, leaving William as head of the family.

William was a very observant, bright, fairly-well educated young man. When he was twenty-five years old, he married Mary Cornwall, a seventeen year-old Loyalist. Thirteen children were born to this union. On September 1, 1823, he purchased all of Pelee Island for $500, becoming the first and only white owner of the whole island. It took eleven years before William had built a home and prepared his family to move. In 1834, he brought along with his wife and children his sister Betsy and his aged mother, Elizabeth Turner McCormick, to establish permanent residence on Pelee. William and his wife Mary both lie at rest in the cemetery donated to the island by their daughter, Anne McCormick.

Before William McCormick moved his family to Pelee Island to make their home, land had been cleared and some stone quarried. There was a light house on the northeast point of Pelee built by the government. In 1834 William became its first keeper. Livestock, horses, cattle, and wild hogs were there.

Water came from wells, hand dug and lined with stone, some of which were more than twenty feet deep. Many of these were used for refrigerating foods, as they didn't freeze in winter, and they were cool in summer.

During the early days, lumber and firewood shipped to the mainland were cash crops. Some of the lumber went to Europe for building. William's sons, Alexander, John, and William, were the workers and overseers for this. In 1836 a saw mill was erected on the spot known as Mill Point on the southeast part of the island.

Before William McCormick had passed on, he made a will giving each of his children 300 acres of land, 100 acres for a school, ten acres for a church and a village, and the rest of the island was to be equally divided among his children.

Alexander wasn't satisfied with his father's will and didn't abide by it. He sold land and timber as he wished, some to a company from Cleveland, Ohio whose agent was a Mr. Whipple. He brought tenants to Pelee and built houses for them. One of these, Henry Price, planted a vineyard of two or three acres which was the forerunner of grape growing on Pelee. Alexander's actions and independence ostracized him from the rest of his family, and he finally moved off the island not to return.

When William McCormick purchased Pelee Island, he had his deed recorded. However, after his death it was discovered that the government hadn't issued a patent. The McCormick's lawyer failed in court to produce a rightful title, and judgment was against the McCormicks. According to this judgment, none of the land which Alexander had sold belonged to the buyers, but all of it to the Government of Canada.

The McCormicks were not willing to let this judgment rest. They employed a lawyer named John Stewart who presented all necessary proof to the court. After reviewing facts presented, Judge Henry J. Bolton handed down the following decision:

"That the former judgment against the McCormicks should be set aside; that the island had never been ceded to the Crown by the Indians; that the Government had never been in possession of it." He recommended that patents be issued to the McCormicks severally, dividing the land as directed by William McCormick's will.

In 1865, Thaddeus Smith, D.J. Williams, and Thomas S. Williams purchased forty acres from the McCormicks on the north end of Pelee. Although the Williamses never lived on the island, Thaddeus Smith moved his family there in 1867. The year before that twenty-five acres of grapes had been planted.

Edward and John Wardroper purchased fifteen acres of land in 1866 and built a home. They, too, were pioneers in growing grapes. Because of ideal soil and climate, vineyards flourished. More and more people came to buy land and to work in the industry. Within a few years a wine cellar was built, and several businesses involved in making and selling Pelee Island wines came into being. However, like the other Lake Erie islands, growing grapes and making wine on Pelee flourished for a few decades but eventually succumbed to California wines and ill fortune.

For awhile fishing, both commercial and sport fishing, lured people to Pelee Island. In the early 1880s, John Maginis from New York City, and Charles Mills from Sandusky, Ohio were instrumental in forming a club for a group of wealthy men from various walks of life. They purchased ten acres of land on the north side of Pelee and erected a club house. The club was limited to twenty-five members, some of whom were General Philip Sheridan, Judge Walter Q. Gresham who was Secretary of State under President Grover Cleveland, J.R. Jones of Chicago who was ex-Minister of Brussels, and Marshall Fields. This was known as The Pelee Club. This group of dignitaries brought some wealth and prosperity to a part of Pelee Island as well as sportsmanship, beauty, and curiosity.

As far as commercial fishing is concerned, as was true around the other Lake Erie islands, fishermen used pound nets to harvest the fish. Thomas L. McCormick was one of these early fishermen. Sturgeon, whitefish, and herring were plentiful. Each day during spring and fall seasons, a tug from the Post Fish

Company of Sandusky, Ohio picked up the fish. When the number of fish in Lake Erie diminished, the Canadian government placed restrictions on the fishermen. The industry had many years of ups and downs and changed hands many times. Gill-netting came and went. Catches of sturgeon, herring, and whitefish changed to catches of perch, pickerel, and catfish. Trap netting helped the supply of pickerel to become almost extinct for a period of time. The government enacted new laws to protect both the fish and the sportsfisherman, driving the commercial fisherman on Pelee Island almost into oblivion.

Much of Pelee was marshland. Lemuel Brown from Cleveland, Ohio came to Pelee in 1878 and purchased six hundred twenty-five acres in the center part of the island. During a dry spell he cultivated and planted the land only to find it two feet under water the next spring. Because of the fertility of the soil, he became obsessed with draining the land.

Lemuel Brown had been a dock builder at Put-in-Bay where he met a Dr. Scudder, founder and owner of Eclectic Medical College of Cincinnati, Ohio. Dr. Scudder had traveled in the Netherlands where he had observed their system of dikes and drainage. He believed this method could be of use at Pelee Island. He and Lemuel Brown purchased over four thousand acres of land, mostly wet lands, from the McCormicks. A parcel of this land on the north shore was set aside for a pumping station.

Steam dredges came to Pelee in 1888 and cut canals at least twelve miles long through the marsh. Ditches led the water to the canals. Marsh water was conducted to the pumping station which sent it into Lake Erie. The marsh was cleared of growth with the help of back-breaking labor and a fire that burned a large area of the marsh. Later this land was sold in twenty to fifty acre plots which yielded many crops of potatoes, wheat, and corn.

Messrs. Dwelle and Lewis of Sandusky, Ohio later arrived on the scene and purchased four hundred fifty acres of the south marsh which they drained and three hundred acres of upland. Making the marshland tillable brought more people to live and work on Pelee Island, and so the community grew.

By 1899, the Municipal Drainage Act of Ontario made it

possible for the island to borrow money and to make the canals deeper. Other pumping stations came into being. The canals were dredged and re-cleaned several times. In 1915, Ralph Harris introduced tile drainage, and nearly all tillable land on Pelee was tiled.

The high level of water in Lake Erie at times, along with some of our violent storms, has been a constant threat of water damage and especially erosion along the shores of Pelee. During a particularly dangerous time in May 1951, flooding was inevitable. Rieger Brothers Construction Company had opened an old stone quarry on the north side of the island. The township purchased stone from them to protect the shores, and in doing so not only prevented much erosion but also saved many of its roads and land.

When growing and harvesting of grapes and making wine had come to a standstill, a new industry came to Pelee—growing and curing tobacco. This thrived, bringing families to the island from the south and from as far away as England. The tobacco era lasted from the turn of the century until the 1920s when a different type of tobacco from that grown on Pelee was in demand.

During the depression, almost all farming ceased. Then some of the farmers became interested in co-operatives and formed a Co-operative Association. They wanted to build a grain elevator but needed to do so at the end of a wharf. Through much work they were instrumental in persuading the Federal government to give enough money to add an extension to Scudder dock, and by July of 1935 their elevator was completed. Following the building of the elevator, many cash farm crops were raised—soy beans, wheat, corn, and even honey for awhile.

When Pelee Island was first settled, there was no school building. Children were taught privately and sent to the mainland for education. However, in 1868 the island became a township, and during the 1870s two schools were built, one known as School Section Number 3 which provided for pupils on the south and west sides and the middle of the island. Soon after, a one-room log school and community hall combined was built on the north side. In 1882, through the generosity of Fred McCormick, a new and larger school was built. In 1888, another school site was purchased where the building now standing was erected.

In 1889, the Ontario Legislature passed an act which divided the township of Pelee into four wards. Old school boards were dissolved and new ones formed. Four new schools were built. In 1913, the one on the south end of Pelee burned when a young girl, Arvilla Thomas, was starting a fire with oil. She lost her life in the fire. Shortly afterward a new school replaced it.

By the turn of the century over a thousand people inhabited Pelee. More and better schools succeeded the old ones. A high school was in operation until 1930 in the Masonic Hall. In 1944, the schools were consolidated into one building. In 1958, it was decided to send pupils in grades eleven, twelve, and thirteen to the mainland for their education. Their expenses, tuition, room, board, and transportation, were taken care of by taxes. This situation created much controversy among taxpayers, many of them feeling it illegal for them to pay board for the pupils. A vote decided the parents pay one-third and taxes two-thirds of the cost. During the 1960s, Pelee was able to get assistance from the government of Ontario to the extent of being reimbursed $3.00 per day for each student sent to the mainland. Just as prosperity in farming and fishing had brought many families to live and work on Pelee Island, unfortunately, education to better their way of life sent them away. Some families refused to be separated from their children and so moved to the mainland to make their home.

The first church on the island existed before 1863, an Anglican Church. As records of its dedication were lost, the exact date of its building isn't known. Someone built a building of Pelee Island stone and next to it a frame building for a rectory.

There was 1.11 acres of land purchased on the southeast end of Pelee in 1883 for a Methodist Church. This building was of frame construction. In 1898, another Methodist Church was dedicated on the north side of the island, this, also, built of stone.

In 1925, the Methodist churches of Canada became United Churches, and in 1942 they came under the Anglican Diocese.

A Roman Catholic Church came into being in 1887, built

about half-way across the island. As there were very few priests who ever lived on the island, it was more of a mission church.

In 1954, Reverend Stahl conducted services of the Pentecostal Church in his home. Later in 1960, a beautiful building was erected for these services.

In addition to farming, there have been other businesses which thrived for awhile on Pelee. Shortly after the turn of the century, quarry operations began and were active for a few years. During the 1950s, building of adequate harbors became a necessity. Going back a few years, in 1896, the first oil well was drilled on a farm then owned by John Finlay. From the drilling of early wells, people were able to pipe gas into their homes for heating and cooking. In 1958, Phillips Petroleum Company cooperated with The Blue Water Gas and Oil Company of London, Ontario in a drilling venture which produced no results and was discontinued.

Over the years many small mercantile stores and hotels have existed for awhile and for various reasons have ceased to exist. As in any other locations, businesses come and go. Probably the best known for these businesses is The Pelee Island Trading Post on the west side. It was opened by Elmer Holl and his wife, who were from the Cleveland, Ohio area.

The government of Pelee came into being in 1868. The Ontario Legislature passed a bill making the island a separate municipality naming it the Township of Pelee Island. Before that it had been a part of Mersea Township. The governing body consisted of three members, two councillors who were to have seats on the county council and a reeve. The first councillors were Walter Grubb and Zenas Quick. Mrs. Arthur McCormick was the first reeve.

In 1917, the council was able to annex Little Middle Island, Old Hen Island, and East Sister Island into the corporation of Pelee.

On January 9, 1939, Captain Flowers introduced to Council the possibility of Pelee having electricity. Councillors Samuel Lucas and H.V. Beard suggested a letter be sent to the Hydro Commission for considering this matter. However, it wasn't until July 20, 1955, that citizens were able to celebrate the electric cable's being connected to the island.

In 1902, there was a cable laid under the water from Point Pelee to Pelee Island to provide telephone and telegraph service. Often during the winter ice would cut the cable, leaving the half dozen telephones that had been installed throughout the island without service until spring. In 1913, a Mr. James brought a crew of men to install a party line system on Pelee. Around 1933, an emergency radio telephone service was completed, making the first cable obsolete. In 1966, Bell Telephone purchased the old Pelee system, re-built the plant, and brought direct-dialing to the island.

On August 13, 1927, Reeve R.C. Barnes reported to council that a Mr. Vorhees of the Department of Conservation of Ohio had donated several English Ring Neck pheasants to the island. Council accepted these and immediately passed laws to protect the birds. By 1931, the birds had reproduced to the point that they were destroying gardens. Council petitioned the Department of Game and Fisheries for permission to kill some of the birds. The Department refused permission. When Game Warden Jensen visited the island in July of 1932 and saw so many pheasants, he recommended a few days of open season. As a result of his recommendation, the first open season in the fall of 1932 reduced the pheasant population by 125 birds. This was the beginning of a valuable source of revenue for both the community and its residents through the sale of hunting licenses and services to the hunter.

The coming of the airplane into Pelee brought about some changes in their way of life. On February 3, 1939, Council received word that the Federal Government would grant $1,500 toward a sixty-five acre landing field, the beginning of their airport. On December 15, 1941, they purchased a small building for shelter at the airport. By September of 1947, they extended the runway eight hundred feet. There is a good air service to and from Pelee. Many flights are made to and from the United States mainland by way of Griffing Flying Service of Sandusky, Ohio, as well as by airlines into Canadian mainland. This invention of the Wright Brothers changed the whole perspective of living on an island in winter and even during navigation season provided quick and emergency services when necessary.

# HULDAH'S ROCK

Many years ago when Indians roamed throughout Canada and the United States, they traveled the waters of Lake Erie at will. At one time some of them went to the St. Lawrence Valley. While there, they captured a beautiful young French girl and fled with her along the river into Lake Erie. Eventually they arrived at Pelee Island.

An Indian chief at Pelee courted the young maiden, who finally consented to be his wife. The two of them produced a beautiful half-breed daughter whom they named *Huldah*. As the mother was seemingly an educated person, she in turn educated her child.

Years passed. One day a young Englishman came to Pelee Island. When he met the beautiful girl living among the Indians there, he was amazed. Soon he fell in love with her and persuaded her to be his wife. For several years the two were happy together.

One day a letter came informing the Englishman that his mother was gravely ill and that he must go to her bedside. When he left his wife, he promised that he would return.

The beautiful girl waited faithfully for her husband for many moons. Then one day she received a letter telling her that he was not coming back. He had found someone else. If she had to live without him, life no longer held any meaning for the half-breed. She went to the northwest shore of Pelee where there was a large rock, climbed to the top of it, and made one final leap into Lake Erie. The rock became known as Huldah's Rock. Although her life came to a tragic end, throughout all these years her rock has probably saved many lives. It serves as a guide for the mariner sailing the sometimes treacherous waters of Lake Erie.

# RAID OF THE PATRIOTS

After the War of 1812, friction developed in Ontario between newly arrived settlers and what we today would refer to as the Establishments. By 1837, this friction had developed to the point of rebellion. Those who rebelled called themselves the Patriots. They were very active along the Detroit River and along the international boundary line, waging their own private war wherever they could. Many of their sympathizers lived in the United States along the Lake Erie borders.

Two of their generals, Marcus Van Rensselear and Donald McCleod, along with a small group of men marched from Navy Island in the Niagara River to Sandusky, Ohio in February of 1838. There they procured men and necessities and planned an invasion of Canada. Their attack was to be launched from the Lake Erie island area. They were to receive ammunition and provisions from Colonel John S. Vreeland at Port Clinton. When they learned that supplies had been sent by mistake to Monroe, Michigan, the Patriots continued on their way across the ice to Pelee Island with outdated weapons and what little provisions they had received from people in Sandusky, Norwalk, and Huron.

William McCormick and his sons had received a warning that the Patriots were headed their way. Quickly they got together their family including William's aged mother, Elizabeth Turner, and crossed over the ice to Canada's mainland. Once there, they immediately informed Fort Malden of these rebels' presence.

That winter a heavy bridge of ice had made crossing from

one island to another fairly easy. This small army of men had visited Kelleys Island where they tried to persuade some of its inhabitants to join them. Failing in their mission, they continued on to Pelee. (See "A Tale of Jake Hay.")

Colonel Maitland, along with Captain Brown, and one company of volunteers and three of Regulars, brought two brass pieces, the cavalry, artillery, and sleighs. William McCormick's son guided them across the ice to Pelee. They arrived at North Pelee early in the morning of March 3, 1838.

When the rebels saw the uniforms and bayonets of the men reflecting the sunlight, they became frightened and hid in the thick woods. The snow was deep, making it difficult for them to make their way to the south of the island, from which they intended to retreat. By the time they reached the south end, Colonel Maitland's men had come down from the north end on sleighs running on the ice.

A letter dated March 3, 1838 to Brigadier-General Brady at Detroit contained this information: "Colonel Maitland has at this moment returned with the troops from Point Au Pelee, having cleared the island of the pirates who were in some force there." It states their loss to have been nine killed, about 40 wounded and 20 prisoners including the former Colonel Seward and Captain Van Rensselaer (nephew of General Van Rensselaer, American associate of William Lyon Mackenzie).

Following the battle, both sides were accused of plundering private property and abusing prisoners. Several Patriots escaped to the mainland of the United States where they were given aid such as food, medical treatment, and shelter. Later, disguised as farmers, they were smuggled to a safe place.

On Pelee Island this battle is referred to as "The Fenian Raid." Others call it "The Battle of the Ice." According to record, it was the last battle fought between the United States and Canada.

# CONCLUSION

As the reader read and compared the different Lake Erie islands, he no doubt saw many similarities in the history of and the tales told about the islands. Although each piece of land stands alone in the great body of water and has a uniqueness of its own, its inhabitants face the same obstacles as those of the other islands do in conquering an isolated way of life. It's rather ironic that as man learns to conquer the obstacles, if he stays long enough, the island conquers him. Should he ever return to inhabit the mainland, his life will never be the same. For most, there will always be a longing to be back on one of the little green spots where waves are lapping on the shore and the radiant sunsets give a bright promise for tomorrow.
The end.